Norfolk Churches

FROM THE AIR

The Royal School of Church Music
Norfolk and Norwich Area

The Dean's Award
for Choristers

Presented to

Aidan Rengert

Of

St. Nicholas, North Walsham

By the Very Revd Dr Jane Hedges
Dean of Norwich
in Norwich Cathedral
on

14 June 2015

First published 2014 by Poppyland Publishing, Cromer, NR27 9AN
www.poppyland.co.uk

Printed in the EU by Latitude Press Ltd

ISBN 978 1 909796 09 6

A catalogue record for this book is available from the British Library.

Designed and typeset in 10 pt on 12 pt Humnst 777

Picture credits

All photographs © 2014 MIke Page

Norfolk Churches

FROM THE AIR

Aerial photography by Mike Page
Text by Pauline Young

POPPYLAND
PUBLISHING

Introduction

There are 217 churches in Norfolk mentioned in the Domesday Book of 1086, and a lot more that aren't listed in Domesday. Of those still standing some 750 were in existence by the middle of 13th century.

Probably the most significant and far reaching event in English church history has been the Reformation. When Henry VIII fell out with the church of Rome over the matter of a divorce from his first wife Catherine of Aragon in the forlorn hope of begetting a son through marriage to a second wife (Anne Boleyn) the existing church was thrown into chaos, largely orchestrated by Henry's chief minister Thomas Cromwell. The 'fall out' created the Church of England.

After the Reformation the Protestantism of Henry's son Edward VI (1547-53) was replaced by the return to Catholicism of Mary (1553-58) daughter of Henry's first wife Catherine of Aragon. There was a return to the Protestant faith with Elizabeth I (1558-1603). The introduction of the Book of Common Prayer 1549 and its revisions were begun during Edward VI's reign and remained in general use until the 20th century. It is used still in some churches for particular services. Successive monarchs made relatively small changes affecting the buildings, except for the long period of Victoria's reign (1837-1901) when many of her loyal subjects seemed intent on modernising, replacing and generally tidying up church interiors – sometimes to the church's detriment.

The interregnum of Oliver Cromwell and his son Richard as Lord Protectors (1653-1658/9) saw the Puritans wreak much destruction. Norfolk and Suffolk seemed to suffer badly with the desecration of 'graven images'. For example on many (but not all – fortunately they missed or chose to miss some) magnificent rood screens, faces were scratched out. Suffolk born William Dowsing was responsible for much destruction in East Anglian churches, any 'easily reachable' target e.g. altar rails, pictures, crucifixes, stone carvings were removed or spoiled (generally stained glass windows were untouched thereby avoiding having to replace them to keep out the weather). But it's reckoned even then that the damage caused by Puritans was rather less than the wholesale removal of Catholic symbols at the Reformation. It wasn't until the Restoration of the monarchy with Charles II (1660-85) that many of the statues, ornate tombs and brass inscriptions we see today were introduced. In general, monuments were commissioned by and in memory of the rich, although the occasional church warden or parson gets a mention. In the churchyard there's a different picture; tombstone inscriptions were available to all who could afford a tombstone, which makes them valuable source material.

We have been so lucky that a readily available building material exists in Norfolk. Flint is exceptionally hard wearing, can be used whole as pebbles or 'knapped', revealing an inside surface with varieties of colour ranging from black, through grey or brown to white, all within one stone. Flint has been used in the majority of our churches with the exception of the grander ones.

Over the centuries the appearance of the church from the churchyard or indeed from an aircraft has hardly changed, it's only once through the door that history unfurls. The door through which we go is usually, but not always, the door in the south porch – sometimes the door is in the base of the tower, sometimes the north side. Mike Page's aerial pictures of some of Norfolk's wonderful churches, there are enough images left over for a second volume, have recorded an almost unchanged scene given the deteriorations due to weather, the additions (a tower here, a porch there, a parapet) and subtractions (towers have had a tendency to fall down over the centuries, likewise abandoned churches). But the special thing about looking at churches, either outside or in, is that each is unique.

The origin of round towers ,of which Norfolk has the largest number in the country, (three quarters of the total country-wide count of 170) continues to be uncertain, but there are plenty in this book, all different. And younger churches (those built after 17th century) have not generally been featured, there are relatively few of them in the country as a whole; most church building was finished by 1650.

The high wings of Mike Page's Cessna 150 aircraft are especially suitable for aerial photography and through Mike's pictures we all have an opportunity to share the view. His picture library contains thousands of images and on line can be viewed at www.mike-page.co.uk.

This work is not another church guide, there are plenty already. The aim has been to share or awaken interest in these wonderful buildings which are part of our landscape.

Mike Page   Pauline Young
Strumpshaw   Wymondham

The Churches

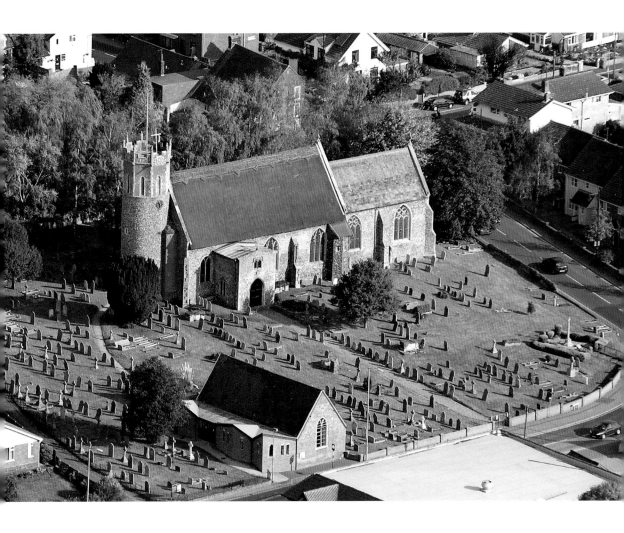

ACLE St Edmund

The Saxon tower was built circa 900, except for the battlements which were added in 1472, and cost, according to the Church Reeve's Commonplace Book, £16. On those battlements stands a statue of St Edmund to whom the church is dedicated. Edmund was King of East Anglia AD855-70. His reign came to an abrupt end when he was beheaded for refusing to denounce Christianity.

Grid Ref: TG 40119 10295
Norwich Road, Acle, NR13 3QQ

ALBURGH All Saints

Pronounced 'Arbrur'. Architectural historian Nikolaus Pevsner (1902-83) considers that the ending of the buttresses just below the bell stage is a mistake which spoils the outline.

Grid Ref: TM 27078 87286
Church Road, Alburgh, IP20 0AB

ALDEBY St Mary

This is a large church for a small village but part of the building up to the Dissolution was a 12th century Benedictine priory. The rest was the parish church. Not all monastic jobs were lost at the Dissolution, the Prior was made Prebendary of Norwich Cathedral. The south porch has a magnificent Norman doorway.

Grid Ref; TM 45048 93312
The Street, Aldeby. NR34 0AB

ARMINGHALL

There was a site where worship took place long before Arminghall church was begun. In 1929 an aerial photograph revealed evidence of a wood henge within the parish, the henge dating back to 3,500BC. Henges (e.g. Stonehenge, Seahenge) are interpreted as places of worship created by early Bronze Age dwellers. The nave and chancel date from the 13th century, the tower a hundred years later.

Grid Ref: TG 25226 04315
Church Close, Arminghall, NR14 8SF

ASHWELLTHORPE All Saints

The double height porch had a Dutch gable added in 18th century making it even higher which is visually in keeping with the nave. The nave seems rather too high for its length. Inside the church the alabaster tomb of Sir Edmund de Thorpe and his wife Joan is the highlight. Sir Edmund died at the Siege of Louviers in France, fighting alongside Henry V.

Grid Ref: TM 14677 97683
The Street, Ashwellthorpe, NR16 1EZ

ATTLEBOROUGH
The Assumption of the Blessed Virgin Mary

What is now the east end of the church was once part of a larger building with a nave and chancel east of the crossing, cruciform in shape. It's unusual for the tower to be at the east end as here. Only the first stage of the original Norman tower has survived, the second stage was added in 12th century. The church once had a tall spire which would have improved the proportions of the whole considerably, but that fell at the end of 17th century.

The rood screen (1475) is the glory of this church – miraculously it survived both the Reformation (1547 onwards) and the Puritans (from 1653). It runs the entire width (52 feet) of the church and there's not another screen to match it for size and completeness. The rood loft is intact, it's 20 feet high. An unusual feature are the heraldic shields forming the loft top. In 1844 a large mural was discovered above and behind the screen. It was painted around 1500 and is one of the most outstanding wall paintings to have survived. A surprising find has been the font which was thrown out by the Reverend Whitwell Elvin when he was rebuilding the extraordinary church at Booton. A sad recent event held here has been the funeral of Peter Beales, the highly respected Royal Horticultural Society Gold Medal rose grower.

Grid Ref: TM04886 95395
Church Street, Attleborough, NR17 2AW

AYLSHAM St Michael

Humphry Repton – influential landscape gardener – whose works include Sheringham Park, Gunton Hall and Woburn Abbey – was buried in this churchyard in 1818. He composed his own memorial which stands against the outside south wall of the chancel.
It reads

'Unmixed with others shall my dust remain;
But mould'ring, blending, melting into Earth'
Mine shall give form and colour to the rose,
And while its vivid blossoms cheer Mankind
Its perfumed colours shall ascend to Heaven'

Clearly an advocate of compost and bone meal then, especially round the roses.

Grid Ref: TG 19241 27015
Church Terrace, Aylsham, NR11 6EU

BANHAM St Mary

St Mary's lead ribbed spire on top of its 14th century tower together standing 125 feet high makes a dramatic impact. On its eastern side where the spire joins the tower is a rare sanctus bell in its leaded 'cote'. Its purpose was to mark the most important part of the communion service and to tell those working in the fields that this was the time for them to pray. Inside the church is a rare wooden effigy of founder Sir Hugh Bardolph. On the west wall hang the royal arms of George III but for good measure in the vestry are the royal arms of Elizabeth I executed in stained glass.

Grid Ref: TM 06344 88222
Church Hill, Banham, NR16 2HN

BARNEY

A lovely little church with bits from 10th century onwards. And what a rational way to deal with the problem of churchyard upkeep!

Grid Ref: TF 99420 32778
The Street, Barney, NR21 0AD

BARNINGHAM WINTER St Mary the Virgin

Not to be confused with Barningham Northwood, also known as North Barningham, a mile away.

The church is in the middle of Barningham Park near to the Hall. The tower, nave and south porch have been in ruins since 17th century and the chancel now serves as a church to which those class conscious Victorians added a small annexe with a servants' entrance.

Grid Ref: TG 14665 35679
Barningham Park, The Street, Matlask, NR11 7HX

BARTON TURF St Michael and All Angels

The church contains possibly the best of all the Norfolk rood screens. These were decorated screens which before the Reformation separated the nave from the chancel. Many remain, even if mutilated when 'graven images' were removed. Thanks to Elizabeth I those screens which had been destroyed were replaced. Included is an amusing depiction of Satan in chains. In the churchyard there's a sadder note – a monument on the south wall of the porch to the four sons of Mr and Mrs Doyley who were all drowned in Barton Broad on Boxing Day 1781.

Grid Ref: TG 34343 21866
Church Road, Barton Turf, NR12 8YU

BAWBURGH St Mary & St Walstan

This, until the Reformation, was a site of pilgrimage to St Walstan one of Norfolk's own saints; a well is nearby with supposedly healing powers. Bawburgh born Walstan was allegedly of royal blood but chose to be a farm labourer at nearby Taverham until his death in 1016. The church roof is unusual in having crow stepped gables, a practice more common in domestic architecture.

Grid Ref: TG 15268 08638
Church Street, Bawburgh, NR9 3NA

BAWSEY St James

Pevsner reports two ruined churches at Bawsey but the remains of its central tower identifies this one as St James's rather than St Michael's. It's been ruined since at least 1745 and may have suffered the same fate as Pudding Norton i.e. peasants driven out by landlords. It was built of a mix of local carstone, iron conglomerate and flint. A Time Team dig of 1998 found a skeleton whose skull had suffered a powerful blow from a sword.

Grid Ref: TF 66248 20796
The Street, Bawsey, PE32 1EU

BEESTON REGIS All Saints

Long before caravans made their appearances all along the coast this church was here. It's even earlier (11th century) than its square tower would suggest. Bits of the church interior came, possibly at the closing of the monasteries, from Beeston Priory. The Priory is now a sad ruin glimpsed across the flower beds of the adjacent Garden Centre. The 15th century rood screen is well worth a visit, the 12 apostles have not been defaced by the iconoclasts in the reign of Edward VI or subsequently during the Civil War.

Grid Ref: TG 17426 43075
Church Close, West Runton, NR27 9QZ

BEIGHTON All Saints

The battlements with their corner figures were put there 1890 but the rest of the tower was built in the 14th century. Part of the nave roof has been sensitively thatched to provide 'hoods' over the clerestory windows.

Grid Ref: TG 38664 08296
Church Hill, Beighton, NR13 3JZ

BELAUGH St Peter

Moor your boat on the bank of the River Bure abeam one of John Betjeman's favourite churches and climb the steep path. You'll find a neat little church, part Norman with a Norman font. The 15th century apostles on the screen had their faces scratched out in 1643 at the start of the Civil War by 'a godly trooper from Hobbies', i.e. nearby Hautbois (today pronounced 'Hobbis').

Grid Ref: TG 28925 18405
Church Lane, Belaugh, NR12 8UY

BERGH APTON St Peter and St Paul

The Victorians had a field day here and restored or added to just about everything in sight with the exception of the 14th century font. But had the Victorians not taken them in hand so many of our churches, those same buildings, might by now have fallen down....which is the greater evil?

Grid Ref: TM 31034 99928
School Road, Thurton, NR15 1BX

BINHAM St Mary

The nave of the church is all that remains of a large Benedictine community. The magnificent west front at the end of the approach footpath gives some idea of the splendid buildings which stood here before the Reformation. Because the priories contained learned, literate men, records exist to date the building accurately – it was begun 1226-44. What is left continues in use as the parish church today.

Grid Ref: TF 98173 39944
Warham Road, Binham, NR21 0DR

BIXLEY St Wandregesilius

The saint's name is said to be a Latinised version of the French St Wandrille, a 7th century Abbot of Fontanelle. The name alone should put Bixley church on the map but sadly it was a victim of arsonists in 2004 and, remotely situated in a small parish, its future looks bleak.

Grid Ref: TG 25523 04936
Bungay Road, Bixley, NR14 8RY

BLAKENEY St Nicholas

Described by Mortlock and Roberts as 'a large powerful building' this was the church of the Carmelite Friars until 1538. The tower is 140 feet high, the shorter tower in the north-east corner of the chancel may have been a lighthouse when Blakeney was a port of some importance with fleets sailing as far as the Arctic in search of fish. This church has almost everything, a royal arms of George III, a Decalogue board plus boards containing the Creed and Lord's Prayer for good measure, a fine 15th century font and an Easter Sepulchre – one of the few in the county.

In the churchyard there's yet another reminder of Blakeney's close association with the sea. John Easter's 1861 tombstone reads:

I with seven others went
Our fellowmen to save
A heavy wave upset our boat
We met a watery grave

Grid Ref: TG 03305 43597
Cley Road, Blakeney, NR25 7UE

BLICKLING St Andrew

The church predated the Blickling Hall by two or three centuries but there had been a previous hall on the site built by Sir Nicholas Dagworth which would have been contemporary with the church. In the south aisle there's a brass of him in full armour with a lion at his feet; he died 1512. The church is rich in brasses which include Anne Astley with her twins in her arms; she died 1512 during childbirth. The brass to Roger and Cecily Felthorp 1454 includes their 16 children. Outside there's a stone on the tower with his personal opinion of tomb inscriptions made by the parish clerk for half a century, one James Howard. He died in 1829, aged 88:

'Praises on tombs is often vainly spent
Mans (sic) good deeds is his best Monument'.

Grid Ref: TG 17869 28457
B1354, Blickling, NR11 6NG

BOOTON St Michael and All Angels

'An extravaganza' is perhaps one of the best ways of describing St Michael and All Angels. It's a riot of styles borrowed from all over the place by the rector for 50 years (1850-1900), the Reverend Whitwell Elvin. The result has been a conversation piece ever since and at the end of it all his wife was complaining that still she was waiting for a new kitchen! John Betjeman writes of the hammerbeam roof that, 'the angels project so far forward that one is not surprised to learn that they were made by a man whose real occupation was the making of figureheads for boats'.

Grid Ref: TG 12289 22389
Church Road, Booton, NR10 4NZ

BRAMERTON St Peter

This church's unusual appearance is due to the extension of the base of the tower to form angled wings – reason unknown. The north transept was added by the Blake family 1860 as was the lych gate 1925 dedicated to Mary Florence Blake and using Norfolk reed and Bramerton grown oak.

Grid Ref: TG29602 04687
The Street, Bramerton, NR14 7DW

BRAYDESTON St Michael

Church monuments are full of social history. As a comment upon infant mortality in the floor there's a ledger slab to Ann Cotton who died in 1727, aged two years six months. Nine of her siblings are laid to rest close by. An adult memorial to fire the imagination is that of Osbert Barney, killed in 1469 by an arrow during the siege of Caister Castle. The striking modern stained glass west window is a memorial to all who fell in the Great War 1914-18.

Grid Ref: TG 33730 08686
Braydeston Hall Lane, Braydeston, NR13 5AP

BUCKENHAM, near Cantley, St Nicholas

The church with its unusual 13th century octagonal tower should be cherished but sadly vandals have wreaked havoc inside. It's now in the care of the Churches Conservation Trust and is being restored.

Grid Ref: TG 35568 05872
Church Road, Buckenham, NR13 4HN

BURGH CASTLE St Peter and St Paul

Most of the tower belongs to 11th century but the red brick top was added in 17th century. Both the tower and the nave wall contain fragments of Roman brick purloined from the 3rd century fort close by. There's a miscellany of styles from various centuries, especially in the window treatments, but most curious of all is the window by the pulpit which commemorates two monarchs separated by 1,000 years. There's a likeness of Queen Victoria 1901 with Windsor Castle in the background and King Alfred 901 with his fleet of ships. The window is in memory of 'Two great Christian monarchs'.

Grid Ref: TG 47649 04974
The Street, Burgh Castle, NR31 9QG

BURGH ST PETER St Mary

It's a bit confusing to have a church dedicated to one saint when there's another saint in the village name. A possible explanation is that there was an earlier church (St Peter's) before the advent of St Mary's. The extraordinary ziggurat tower except for the base (early 16th century) was built by the Reverend Samuel Boycott in 1793.

Grid Ref: TM 49355 93703
The Street. Burgh St Peter, NR34 0DD

BURNHAM OVERY St Clement

This church looks rather 'bitty'. Its central tower built about 1300 has a parapet built 200 years later. The parapet is carved with biblical figures needing binoculars to appreciate them fully. The books say the church was bigger and grander in the past.

The Burnhams each have a church of their own, except for Burnham Market which has two. There's Burnham Deepdale and Burnham Norton, both with their round towers, but best known of all is Burnham Thorpe where Horatio Nelson was born whilst his father was rector there.

Grid Ref: TF 84312 42934
B1155 Burnham Overy, PE31 8HX

BURNHAM WESTGATE St Mary

Burnham Westgate is one of the three parishes of Burnham Market comprising Burnham Westgate, Burnham Sutton and Burnham Ulph. Westgate was the westernmost street of Burnham Westgate. Sutton was the 'south tun' or southernmost dwelling and Ulph signified wolves in the area – all words of Scandinavian origin. The parapet is uniquely carved with biblical figures.

Grid Ref: TF 83020 42092
Church Walk, Burnham Market, PE31 8EB

BURNHAM ULPH All Saints

Within Burnham Market there are three parishes comprising Burnham Westgate, Burnham Sutton and Burnham Ulph. The latter, seemingly stranded on an 'island' between two roads, is thought to be the oldest. When Burnham Sutton church was demolished the church at Burnham Ulph became Burnham Sutton cum Ulph.

There's no tower here but an 18th century bell cote. Although it gives the appearance of having been built in the last two centuries there's a slim Saxon window midway along the south wall of the nave.

Grid Ref: TF 83550 42254
North Street, Burnham Market, PE31 8UR

CANTLEY St Margaret

For many Cantley is synonymous with the sugar beet processing factory (the first in England built 1928) but this rural village on the river Yare has been here rather longer than that. The church was established by the 14th century. In the chancel floor there's a memorial to a hunting man, Robert Gilbert, who died in 1714:

That subtle FOX DEATH
Earth'd him here at last
And left a fragrant scent, so sweet behind,
That ought to be persu'd by all Mankind

Grid Ref: TG 38164 84144
Church Road, Cantley, NR13 3SS

CASTLE ACRE St James

The priory (foreground) is a Reformation ruin but the church survives. Probably it came three centuries later than the priory foundation. The church contains a wonderful 26 feet high, 15th century font cover, a splendid 'wine glass' pulpit, a rood screen of twelve saints with St Andrew peppered with lead shot (from the Civil War?) and some bench ends with animal carvings and misericords. Misericord came from the Latin 'misericorda' meaning 'act of mercy' and they were originally from monasteries. The monks could lean on them whilst appearing to be standing during long services. There's a lions head, an angel and an eagle. But most noteworthy of all is the priest's door on the south side of the chancel – there's now a filled-in arch which originally would have been 14 feet high and dating from 12th or 13th century. There's speculation that this would have been built to accommodate a knight on horseback so that he and his horse could enter the church and be blessed before battle.

Grid Ref: TF 81589 15022
South Acre Road, Castle Acre, PE32 2AB

CASTLE RISING St Lawrence

A magnificent 12th century Norman church but the Victorian 'improvers' left their mark here too. On the opposite side of the road stands the Hospital of the Holy and Undivided Trinity (1614) where twenty female almshouse residents still wear their red cloaks and black pointed hats to attend church. Off picture is the gigantic mound and ruin of the castle to which Edward III's mother Queen Isabella was banished in 1330.

Grid Ref: TF 81589 15022
The Street, Castle Rising, PE31 6AG

CAWSTON St Agnes

Built on wool fortunes, this church has many magnificent features such as the vast west window in the tower, the west doorway with a wodwose (wild man) and dragon, the hammerbeam roof with an abundance of angels (take your binoculars) and the Mediaeval rood screen containing representations of 16 saints – it's St Jerome who merits a special visit, he's wearing spectacles!

Grid Ref: TF 13393 23848
Church Lane, Cawston, NR10 4AJ

CHEDGRAVE All Saints

Pevsner describes this as 'a very irregular church' (he means the shape rather than any 'goings on') and certainly the Norman tower is both in an unusual place and in having a thatched cap. Another interesting feature is the glazing of the east window part of which was purchased by Lady Beauchamp Proctor of Langley from Rouen Cathedral in 1797. This would have been towards the end of the French Revolution and possibly not a good time for any aristocrat to be setting foot on French soil.

Grid Ref: TM 36330 99375
The Street, Chedgrave, NR14 6NH

CLAXTON St Andrew

There's a 'miscellaneous' look to the outside of this church – it's attractive in an honest to goodness way, probably because it was built over several centuries. The thatched nave is part Norman, the tower 14th century with red brick Tudor corners, the porch is Tudor too but the chancel is pure Victorian. The 'hutch' on top of the tower provides access.

Grid Ref: TG 32786 03196
Church Lane, Rockland St Mary, NR14 7HZ

CLEY NEXT THE SEA St Margaret

When Cley was one of the (now silted up) Glaven ports with ships sailing as far as Iceland for fish, the church was a landmark and a light was kept burning in the tower. This is a big church and the clerestory windows are both magnificent and unusual alternating between cinqefoil and two light windows. During building, the Black Death (1349) decimated the community and the part creation of the south transept was abandoned leaving the unfinished building that remains today.

Grid Ref: TG 04841 43126
Holt Road, Cley, NR25 7TT

COLNEY St Andrew

The round tower is probably Saxon, most of the rest is probably early 14th century. The inscription of 1806 over the porch entrance remains relevant today. It's an epitaph for seventy nine year old John Fox who was killed on this spot 'having been thrust down and trampled on by the horses of a waggon' (sic). The inscription ends

READER if thou drivest a team be careful and endanger not the life of another or thine own'.......

and that's still relevant even now the new Norfolk and Norwich University Hospital is just round the corner.

Grid Ref: TG 18072 07955
Old Watton Road, Colney, NR4 7UF

CROMER St Peter and St Paul

This is the highest tower in Norfolk at 160 feet. The church dominates the town and from the sea makes an impressive landmark. The chancel dates from 1880 but the rest of the church is restored 15th century with some 20th century windows. Cromer has not always been on the coast. The hamlet of Shipden existed further into the sea until 13th century and as late as 1880 a ship was in collision with a submerged part of Shipden church tower at Church Rock. Memorials inside the church include one to Cromer's most famous and distinguished son, Henry Blogg, the most highly decorated lifeboatman ever. He was coxswain of the Cromer lifeboat for over 50 years and when he died in 1954 aged 78 crowds lined the streets to pay their respects as the funeral cortege passed.

Grid Ref: TG 21962 42205
Church Street, Cromer, NR27 9HH

CROSTWIGHT All Saints

By 1910 the top of the tower had become dangerous. It was removed and capped in red tile. The 14th century wall paintings were discovered in 1846; here are the seven deadly sins (pride, anger, covetousness, lust, gluttony, envy and sloth) in the form of a tree and a picture of St Christopher. It was common practice to paint his image on the wall opposite the church's main entrance on the theory that no harm could come to anyone who had seen Christopher's image on the day of a journey. He was patron saint of travellers and generally is depicted spanning a river with the Christchild either on his shoulder or in his hand.

Grid Ref: TG 33398 29990
Hall Road, Crostwight, NR28 9NP

DENTON St Mary

The Saxo-Norman round tower collapsed 18th century and its replacement, a combination of brick and stone, is rather striking. The flint top was not added until 1843 in the century of general restoration which included flooring the interior with Minton tiles. On the orders of Queen Elizabeth I the royal arms were to be displayed in every parish church but Denton goes three better. Apart from the Arms of George III over the south door and Victoria's over the north there are Tudor and Stuart Arms in the east window.

Grid Ref: TM 28621 87348
Danacre Road, Denton, IP20 0AA

DERSINGHAM St Nicholas

Much of this 14th century church is built of the mellow carstone found in the west of the county. Being close to Sandringham some royal input is unsurprising – there's a carving on the rood screen created by a craftsman of the queen's woodcarving school at Sandringham of 1917 and the royal arms over the North Door came from the front of a local grocer's shop which previously had held the royal patent.

Grid Ref: TF 69302 30386
Manor Road, Dersingham, PE31 6YW

DISS St Mary

The early 14th century tower has a processional way through it. On the eastern end of the nave, above the clerestory windows, is a sanctus bell turret. The bell was tolled at the consecration of the bread and wine during Holy Communion (called Mass before 16th century) so that people in the street could make the sign of the cross and feel themselves part of the service. The Manning family were rectors here in an unbroken line 1778-1916.

Grid Ref: TM 11719 80023
Church Street, Diss, IP22 4JT

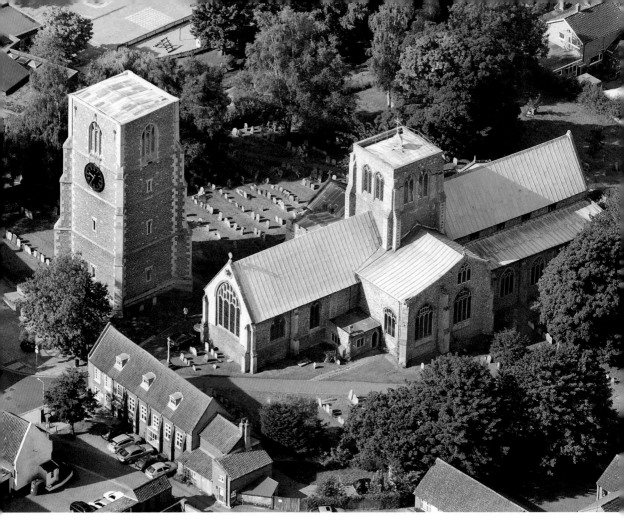

EAST DEREHAM St Nicholas

The separate, stark tower without a parapet was built specifically to house the clock and bells. In the churchyard is St Withburga's well; she was a local saint who established a nunnery here at Dereham 645AD. There's a Seven Sacrament font, the tallest in East Anglia for which the mason received £10 in 1468. There's also a memorial to the poet William Cowper who died in 1700.

Grid Ref: TF 98704 13305
Church Street, Dereham, NR19 1DN

EAST HARLING St Peter and St Paul

This church is elegant inside and out and with magnificent tombs of the Harling and Lovell families. Sir Robert Harling was killed in battle in Paris in 1435; his brass inscription describes his death as

'at length mangled by force of arms'

The east window of beautiful 15th century glass, was hidden in the manor house attics during the Civil War, returned to the church in 1736, removed again at the start of the Second World War and finally restored in 1947.

Grid Ref: TL 98995 86684
Church Road, East Harling, NR16 2NA

EAST RAYNHAM St Mary

The church was almost entirely rebuilt in 1868 but is a copy of the original. The chancel was paid for by the rector and the nave by the Marquess Townshend at a total cost of £7,000.

Grid Ref: TF 87964 25544
The Street, West Raynham, NR21 7ER

EASTON St Andrew

Time has not treated this little church very well. The tower fell in the 18th century and hasn't been replaced and the south wall of the nave has a cement coating which is not very pretty (see also Raveningham). The chancel is a Victorian rebuild of 1883. The porch is high for its width and suggests a possibility at some time of an upper room. Very curious is the small clerestory window above the porch; usually the windows run the length of the nave. The pulpit with linenfold panelling and attractive flower carvings was brought here from the redundant St Mary, Coslany, Norwich.

Grid Ref: TG 12999 10971
The Street, Easton, NR9 5DF

EATON St Andrew

A successful combination of ancient and modern. The original church dates from 13th century, the tower 15th century and the modern addition from 1996. It's a fitting transition entering the modern through the old. This is the only Norwich church which has a (part) thatched roof.

Grid Ref: TG 20256 05969
St Andrews Drive, Eaton, NR4 6NH

EDGEFIELD St Peter and St Paul

In 1876 the Rev Canon Walter Marcon returned to Edgefield on the death of the incumbent, his father. He found both the church fabric and the enthusiasm of the congregation in need of restoration. With the exception of the old tower he moved the remains of the church to a new site in the village . The building was completed in 1885 with the exception of the curiously placed new tower which was finished in 1908. He died in 1936 in the room in which he had been born.

Grid Ref: TG 09361 34197
Church Lane, Edgefield, NR24 2AF

EDINGTHORPE All Saints

The round tower with an octagonal top (the lower part AD900-1050) was, like Tasburgh, built on an elevated site within a double bank implying that it was on the site of a prehistoric hill fort. The 14th century rood screen (with the almost regulation Roundhead bullet holes) contains six superbly painted saints and to complement them a wall painting of St Christopher, uncovered in the 1930s. The lych gate was erected by the Reverend Harvey Muriel in memory of those young men who died in the Great War, including his own son B J Muriel. His ship was torpedoed in the Mediterranean 1915.

Grid Ref: TG 32332 33151
Church Lane, Edingthorpe, NR28 9TN

ELSING St Mary

This church looks so neat because it was built 'all of a piece' in the Decorated order of architecture in about 1330 and the nave is the widest pillarless space in East Anglia at 39 feet across. Inside is a wonderful carved wooden font canopy.

Grid Ref: TG 05171 16542
Church Street, Elsing, NR20 3EA

FAKENHAM St Peter and St Paul

A large church befitting a Norfolk market town. The headstones north of the
church have been removed providing a green open space. The town's fire
engine used to be stored in the space under the tower.

Grid Ref: TF 91919 29702
Market Place, Fakenham, NR21 9BX

FELBRIGG St Margaret

Now part of the National Trust's estate, the house and original village (mostly now disappeared) were named after Sir Simon de Felbrigg who, together with his wife, is commemorated in a large (nine feet long, four feet wide) brass on the aisle floor of the church. Both the church (14th century) and Sir Simon (1416) predate the existing house of 1620.

Grid Ref: TG 19747 39012
Felbrigg Hall, Felbrigg, NR11 8PR

FLITCHAM St Mary

It is said that St Felix, bringer of Christianity to East Anglia, built a church here in the 7th century. The existing church is of Norman origin. The remaining foundations of a chancel would have made the existing tower into a crossing tower but instead its base unusually now serves as a chancel. The 13th century transept is in ruins.

Grid Ref: TF 72511 26632
Church Road, Flitcham, PE31 6BU

FRAMINGHAM EARL St Andrew

It is described by Mortlock and Roberts as a 'pretty little church'. The tower is Norman as is the nave although there have been several 'improvements' over the centuries. All the better for not having been improved is the chancel arch which is undoubtedly Norman, whilst the chancel is Anglo Saxon. A treasure.

Grid Ref: TG 27747 02757
Yelverton Road, Framingham Earl, NR14 7SD

FRAMINGHAM PIGOT St Andrew

Consecrated 1859 and costing £4,500 the church replaced an earlier one. The nave and chancel are faced with square knapped flints. The tower, placed unusually in the north-west corner, is of stone with an octagonal lantern. The four 'lucarne' windows (small openings in the spire to let in light) face in the directions of the cardinal points of the compass. Electric lighting was not installed until the 1950s, two oil lamps remain on the chancel walls as a reminder of previous times.

Grid Ref: TG 27787 03599
The Street, Framingham Pigot, NR14 7QH

FRITTON St Edmund (near Great Yarmouth)

The round tower has Roman tiles at the base. There's a little trap door under the eaves on the south side of the chancel traditionally called the 'Smugglers Loft', ('baccy for the Parson, brandy for the squire' etc). In 1967 a wall painting of St Edmund was revealed, probably of 12th century origin. There's a three decker pulpit (bottom stage for the clerk who lead the responses and conducted the singing, the service was read from the second tier and the minister climbed to the top tier to deliver the sermon). There are only 11 Three Decker Pulpits in the county.

Grid Ref: TG 47327 03599
Church Lane, Fritton, NR31 9EZ

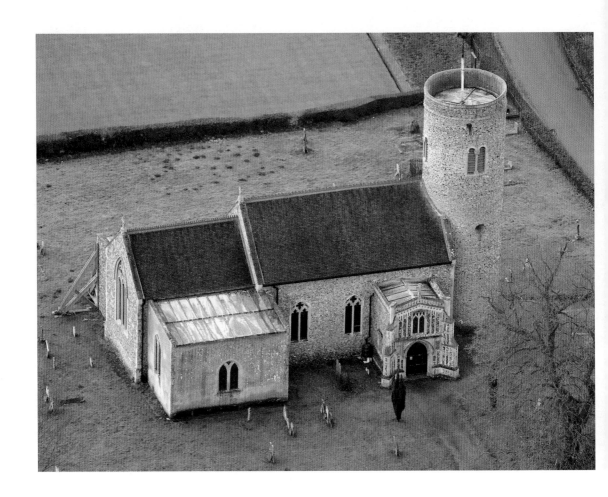

GISSING St Mary

This is considered to be one of the best of the round tower churches – and one of the oldest. The tower is Saxo-Norman with a Saxon round window at lower level and higher up Norman two light windows. The north porch was added in 15th century and its flint flushwork is spectacular. Magnificent too is the double hammerbeam roof and the many angels thereon, the highest ones (should that be 'angels on high?') have wings more outspread than the lower ones.

Grid Ref: TM 14616 85298
Lower Street, Gissing, IP22 5UH

GORLESTON St Andrew

Over the centuries the church has had several restorations, the last serving as a memorial to the Gorleston lifeboatmen who lost their lives in the Second World War. The churchyard was cleared of tombstones by the incumbent vicar in 1800. It's alleged that he sold one to a local baker who used the stone for an oven floor and that the baked loaves bore the impression 'age 75 years'.

Grid Ref: TG 52442 04406
Church Lane, Gorleston, NR31 6LS

GREAT HAUTBOIS St Mary

With their usual zeal and energy the Victorians 'ruinated' this church before building Holy Trinity a quarter of a mile away in 1864. The graveyard is still in use and the chancel roof was left on so that the building could serve as a mortuary chapel.

Grid Ref: TG 26554 23745
The Street, Great Hautbois, NR10 5DF

GREAT MELTON All Saints

The tower is all that remains of St Mary's and the adjacent All Saints was virtually a ruin until its restoration in the 1880s.

Grid Ref: TG 14057 06152
Market Lane, Great Melton, NR9 3BH

GREAT WITCHINGHAM
The Assumption of the Blessed Virgin

The church is 14th century; the eight windowed clerestory (15th century) actually has only seven windows, the westernmost is a dummy! Unusually the south porch has Victorian gates. Inside, the Seven Sacrament font retains some of the colour with which all churches were filled before the Reformation. The royal arms of Charles II over the south door were installed at the Restoration of the Monarchy 1660.

Grid Ref: TG 10372 20057
Church Farm Lane, Great. Witchingham, NR9 5PL

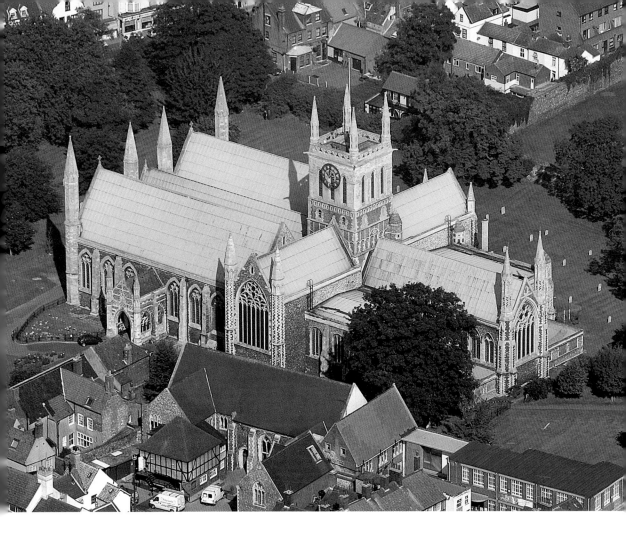

GREAT YARMOUTH St Nicholas

England's largest parish church. Badly bombed on the night of June 24th 1942, the restoration includes the Colman window showing steam drifters in Yarmouth harbour.

Grid Ref: TG 52446 08036
Church Plain, Great. Yarmouth, NR30 1NW

HADDISCOE St Mary

The distinctive round Saxon tower with its 15th century chequerwork battlements is a landmark. Within the porch there's a splendid Norman doorway with a rare Norman sculpture of a priest above. In the church itself there's a wall plaque to painter Sir John Arnsby Brown 1866-1955, who often included the church in his pictures. On the south wall in the churchyard there's a eulogy to William Salter, Yarmouth Stage Coach driver who died in 1776 aged 59. The fourteen-line verse ends:

'And now his faults are all forgiv'n
Elija like drive up to Heaven
Take the reward of all his Pains
And leave to other hands the Reins'

Grid Ref: TM 43929 96898
Church Lane, Haddiscoe, NR14 6PB

HALES St Margaret

The fabric of this Norman church has remained more or less unaltered for 900 years. The rounded apse contains Norman arcading (blank 'windows'). Inside there are wall paintings from different periods including a 15th century St Christopher. Before the Reformation it was common practice to decorate the walls with biblical references, possibly for the benefit of an illiterate congregation. St Margaret's is in the care of the Churches Conservation Trust.

Grid Ref: TM 38348 96104
Church Lane, Hales, NR14 6QN

HAPPISBURGH St Mary

The 110 feet tall tower has been a shipping landmark for centuries, a service much needed for ships in the treacherously shallow North Sea. Several more church towers along the coast, Cromer, Winterton and Blakeney for example, fulfilled the same function. Storms have taken their toll over the centuries and the sea bed must be littered with boats which have broken up on sandbanks or sunk without trace. Buried in this churchyard are 32 bodies from the naval vessel *Peggy*, wrecked on Happisburgh Beach in 1770 together with 119 of the 550 crew of HMS *Invincible* which foundered on Hammonds Knoll in 1801, the bodies having been washed onto the beach. Six other bodies were washed up further along the coast and buried in Winterton churchyard . The *Invincible's* crew were buried in the vicar's glebe lands. The mass grave is not marked except for a memorial in the churchyard erected there 1988; the stone was in part provided by a later HMS *Invincible* .

Grid Ref: TG 37975 31151
Church Street, Happisburgh, NR12 0PL

HARGHAM All Saints

In 18th century part of the tower fell taking with it most of the nave. The church has been stripped of many of its treasures but it is not entirely unloved. An Attleborough builder and his wife took pity on the church, cleared the churchyard and replaced the roof at their own expense. The church had already been stripped almost bare of furnishings but the font remained and in 1982 the couple's infant daughter was christened there. The building is now in the care of the Norfolk Churches Trust.

Grid Ref: TM 01986 91353
Hargham Hall, Hargham, NR16 2JN

HAVERINGLAND St Peter

St Peter's is described as now being in a sort of No Man's Land standing as it does in the midst of the disused Second World War airfield, RAF Swannington. The tower is Norman with the exception of a ground level window but the remainder was rebuilt in the middle of 19th century and has a distinctly different appearance to the mellow tower.

Grid Ref: TG 15140 20910
Haveringland, NR10 4SU

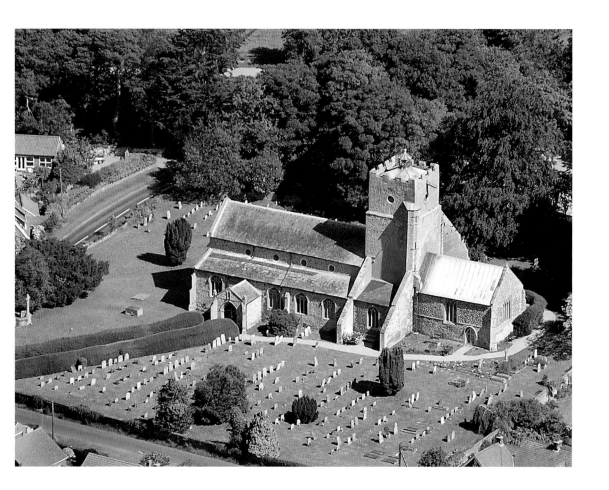

HEACHAM St Mary

This is a big church that was once even bigger. The fabric includes flint, carstone, brick and tile. Inside there are six hatchments of the Rolfe family. Hatchments were diamond shaped boards displaying the coat of arms of the family, carried at the funeral then eventually displayed in the church. And there's a reminder of the story of John Rolfe who in 1616 is reputed to have brought his American Indian princess bride Pocahontas to Heacham; there's a modern monument to her in the church. Sadly she died on board ship off Greenwich three years later, on her way back to America with Sir Walter Raleigh's last expedition.

Grid Ref: TF 68143 37969
Church Lane, Heacham, PE31 7HJ

HECKINGHAM St Gregory

Like its near neighbour at Hales the church is Norman and almost untouched except that the base of the round tower had an octagonal 25 feet added later, making 39 feet in all. The south doorway (inside the porch) is so similar to that at Hales that it's assumed it was by the same craftsman. The church is looked after by the Churches Conservation Trust.

Grid Ref: TM 38439 98843
Church Lane, Heckingham, NR14 6QT

HETHEL All Saints

The chancel was extended northwards early in 18th century to provide a mausoleum for the Branthwaite family – but strangely only two members were ever buried there. Visually the extension is an uncomfortable addition. Alongside a footpath from the church stands the 700 year old Hethel Thorn in what is the smallest (0.025 hectare) Wildlife Trust Nature Reserve in the country.

Grid Ref: TG 17116 00400
Church Lane, Hethel, NR14 8HE

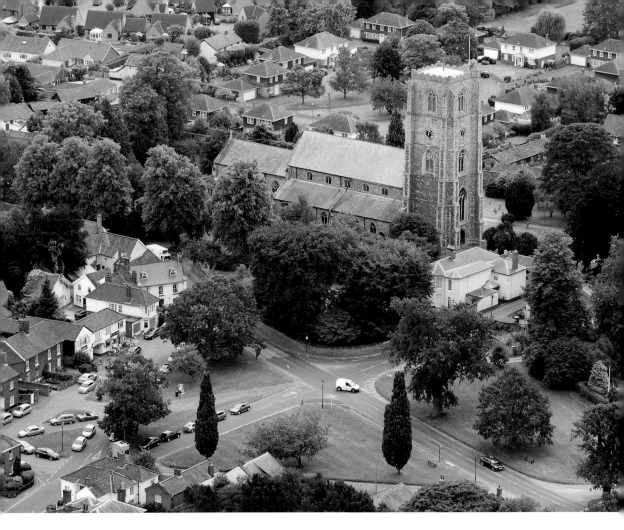

HINGHAM St Andrew

This is a large church with a 120 feet high tower – not the tallest in Norfolk, Cromer's is 40 feet higher) but impressive none the less. Among the many monuments stands a bust of Abraham Lincoln, America's 16th President, whose ancestors came from Hingham.

Grid Ref: TG 02165 02126
Attleborough Road, Hingham, NR9 4HL

HOLKHAM St Withburga

The church stands on a pagan burial mound. There's an unusual 'floor plan'. Entry is via the tower, foundations of an earlier one probably belonging to a Saxon church were found in the nave. There are also two chancels. Altogether a bit of a muddle but pleasing to the eye.

Grid Ref: TF 87797 43628
The Street, Holkham, NR23 1RW

HONINGHAM St Andrew

The lych gate is one of the smallest in East Anglia and is inscribed with one of the common texts, 'Blessed are the dead which die in the Lord.' – 'Lich' is Anglo Saxon for corpse, (German 'leiche'), the body is carried through the lych gate into the church for the burial service. At the top of the tower's pinnacles are seated representations of the four evangelists. At the front of the churchyard the ongoing problem of ground maintenance has been resolved by arranging the tombstones standing to attention in line.

Grid Ref: TG 11419 11247
A47, Honingham, NR9 5BT

HOPTON St Margaret

Hopton's had an identity crisis, sometimes in Suffolk, sometimes in Norfolk. It's in Norfolk now. The earlier church with giant anchor in the churchyard was deemed to be too close to the sea for safety but when it burned down in the

mid 1800s a golden opportunity arose to create a new church further inland. The present one was built in 1865 at the height of Victorian expansion and enthusiasm. The design is striking and access to the belfry is via the small conical tower.

Grid Ref: TM 53016 99977
Coast Road, Hopton, NR31 9ST

83

HORSEY All Saints

The 15th century octagonal top of the Norman round tower is the haunt of owls and harriers. The interior with the underside of the thatch on view has more the feel of a tithe barn.

Grid Ref: TG 45784 23036
Binsley Close, Horsey, NR29 4EF

HOWE St Mary

The tower, except for the conical tile cap, was built some time during the three centuries before the Norman Conquest. The interior has been modernised but the stone corbels of the wall posts (the wall posts take the weight of the roof) have praying angels on all but two. The other two corbels have representations of a crowned king and a lady with a fashionable headdress of circa 1450, her headdress has been likened to a skull cap with Bunny Girl ears.

Grid Ref: TM 27503 99960
Howe Green, Howe, NR15 1HD

KESWICK All Saints

This is the Keswick near Norwich, not the remains of the Keswick on the coast near Mundesley whose church was claimed by the sea during a storm in 1382.

In 1598 the new lord of the manor demolished part of this church to provide building material for the church at Intwood, his adjacent manor. It wasn't until 1893 that John Henry Gurney built a mortuary here which in 1922 was returned to use as a church, albeit a small one the nave being six yards long and seven yards wide. The semicircular apse was added in the 1950s and incorporates a war memorial. Whilst all these changes were taking place the Saxon tower stood steadfast.

Grid Ref: TG 21383 04715
B1113, Keswick, NR4 6TP

KETTERINGHAM St Peter

This is a cosy scene, church and Hall, a few cottages in a picturesque woodland setting. What could be more tranquil in rural 19th century Norfolk? Wrong! Here over several decades a power struggle was waged between the reforming Squire, Sir John Boileau and the conservative parson, the Reverend William Wayte Andrew. But that was a long time ago and now they're sharing the churchyard, hopefully resting in peace. The church has a few angels, some remarkable stained glass and plenty of memorials. The hall, rebuilt in 19th century and now offices, was for 1942– 45 the headquarters of the 2nd US Air Division of the 8th USAAF in Norfolk.

Grid Ref: TG 16382 02564
Church Road, Ketteringham, NR18 9RS

KING'S LYNN St Margaret

When the church and neighbouring Benedictine priory were built in 12th century the town was known as Bishop's Lynn – the Bishop of Norwich owned the marshy land on which they stood. Llyn or lindo was Celtic for lake. Royal status was acquired in 1536 when the town was snatched from the bishopric and became King's Lynn or Lynn Regis. During the Civil War Lynn was staunchly Royalist. It's assumed that building stone from Northamptonshire quarries was transported along what is now the river Great Ouse for the building of the church. Until 1741 the squat middle tower housed a spire and lantern, but they blew down in a gale.

Grid Ref: TF 61771 19803
Saturday Market Place. King's Lynn, PE30 5DQ

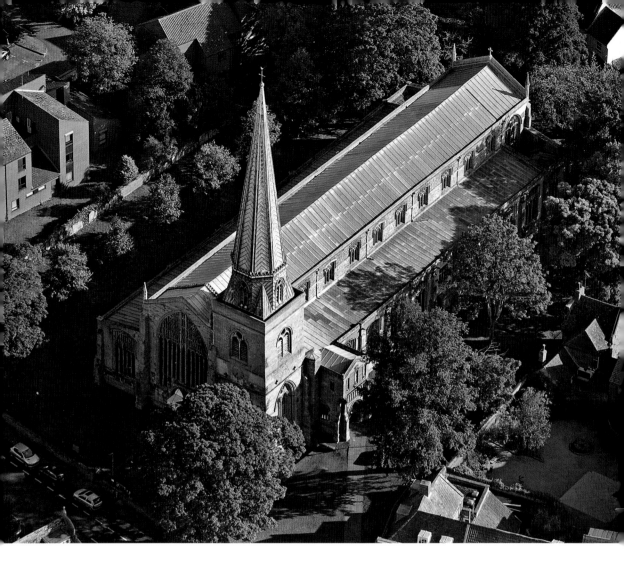

KINGS LYNN St Nicholas

St Nicholas' church has been described as 'more striking than beautiful' and its status is as a 'chapel of ease' to St Margaret's rather than as a church in its own right. Since 1869 the 13th century tower has carried a spire designed by Sir George Gilbert Scott Snr. On the floor near the font is an engraved ledger stone memorial to Robinson Crusoe, son of Robinson and Alice Crusoe. The child died age ten in 1773. Daniel Defoe wrote his adventures of Robinson Crusoe in 1704. The chapel, the largest in England, is in the care of the Churches Conservation Trust and used as concert venue.

Grid Ref: TF 61847 20458
Pilot street, King's Lynn, PE30 1NH

KIRBY BEDON St Andrew

The Victorians more or less rebuilt the entire church except for the South Door, which is Norman but hidden behind a tree in this picture! There's a mausoleum holding the remains of Sir Robert John Harvey who shot himself circa 1870 after the collapse of Norwich's Crown Bank. Part of the late Norman round tower is all that is left of St Mary's church – it was abandoned circa 1660.

Grid Ref: TG 27854 05443
The Street, Kirby Bedon, NR14 7DX

KNAPTON St Peter and St Paul

Here's one of the best hammerbeam roofs in Norfolk (1504) – angels galore, the count varies between 138 and 160. The lowest row was added in 1930 and to many minds those recent members of the angelic host seem somewhat threatening. Is it pure imagination or does even the eagle on the lectern look rather apprehensive?

Grid Ref: TG 30748 34178
Pond Lane, Knapton, NR28 0SF

LESSINGHAM All Saints

It is described as, 'a tiny unpretentious church marooned in fields up a narrow lane'. In 1961 the chancel collapsed in a storm and a new east wall now finishes off the nave. The tower was built over a period of time hence its 'layered' look. There's a Jacobean pulpit circa 1650 with a 'tester' (a sounding board) above.

Grid Ref: TG 40333 28412
Church Lane, Eccles by the Sea, NR12 0SH

LIMPENHOE St Botolph

The neat and tidy appearance of the whole church building is due to an almost complete makeover in 1880 – those energetic Victorians again, one of whom had the nous to rescue a Flemish tapestry from neighbouring Southwood church when Southwood was abandoned at about the same time.

Grid Ref: TG 39527 03994
Church Road, Limpenhoe, NR13 3JB

LITTLE SNORING St Andrew

The round tower belongs to a previous church on this site and stands about six feet away from the present church. Its conical cap resembling a dove cote was added about 1800. The church is a miscellany of architectural styles starting with the Norman. Nearby RAF wartime station Little Snoring used the church for worship and recorded victories on boards here. Also on record is a ledger (floor) slab to the memory of a parish priest, 'as good perhaps as ever lived'.

Grid Ref: TF 95304 32565
The Street, Little Snoring, NR21 0HZ

LITTLE WALSINGHAM St Mary

Fire gutted this church on the night of July 14th-15th 1961 leaving only the tower and south porch intact but it's been superbly restored. The Seven Sacrament font (Pevsner: 'Almost the perfect Norfolk font') was rescued. On the north wall of the chancel is a Jacobean tablet showing the front of a four poster bed with drawn curtains and the inscription 'Dormitorium Edwardi de Fotherbye 1632', 'Here sleeps Edward of Fotherbye 1632.'

Grid Ref: TF 93510 36499
Church Street, Little Walsingham, NR22 6BL

LODDON Holy Trinity

It's surprising that Simon Jenkins doesn't include Holy Trinity in his list of *England's Thousand Best Churches* because it's magnificent and an excellent example of the Perpendicular style. The 30 clerestory windows, the crenellated tower of 1500 with two coffin stones at its base commemorating the two masons who fell to their deaths during the tower's construction, the double height south porch and intricate flint flushwork – all a tribute to the mason's skill. And that's just outside. Inside the church is a hammerbeam roof, a Seven Sacrament font, a Jacobean pulpit, an unusual rood screen depicting scenes rather than saints, a 17th century communion rail (communion rails originally were intended to keep out dogs) and brasses galore, including one for Henry Hobart of Hales Hall who built this church circa 1480. It was the third church on this site.

Grid Ref: TM 36349 98724
Market Place, Loddon, NR15 6EY

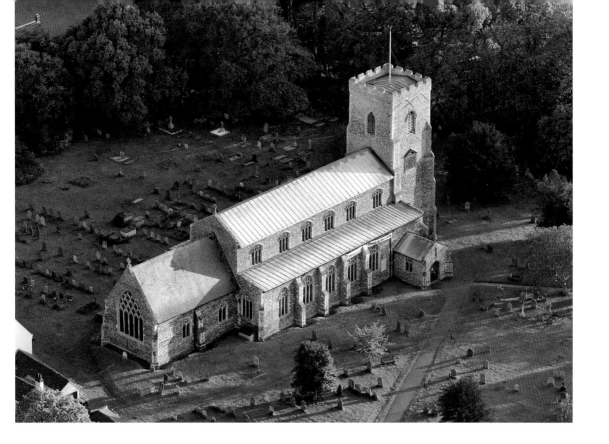

LUDHAM St Catherine

All that remains of the Abbey dedicated to St Benet (Benedict) across the marshes from Ludham are the ruins of a gatehouse containing a later tower mill and some footings. Until the sacking of the monasteries, they were the religious buildings of Benedictine monks. Because of its proximity successive Bishops of Norwich (who became Priors of the Abbey also) spent much time at Ludham, which explains the grandeur of this particular church. All the furnishings are sumptuous but what makes St Catherine's particularly noteworthy is that the church contains within it a record of the events which changed English ecclesiastical history. After Henry VIII sent the monks of St Benet's packing (this momentous event was actually masterminded by Thomas Cromwell) all trappings of the church of Rome began to be removed. Henry's son Edward VI sent out injunctions that all images were to be destroyed, all processions ceased and all candles forbidden. But when Edward died and his Catholic half sister Mary became queen the situation was reversed (except that the monks didn't return). It was not until her half sister Elizabeth, daughter of Anne Boleyn, came to the throne that the reforms begun by Henry VIII and continued by Edward were again implemented. At Ludham the picture of Christ and Mary and John over the rood screen which had been installed on the orders of Mary, but painted on canvas instead of carved in wood because of lack of funds, was left in place . On the reverse, facing into the chancel, the coat of arms of the new monarch (Elizabeth I) were hung there. The canvas remains today.

Eric Edwards, the popular reed cutter, was buried in the churchyard recently.

Grid Ref: TG 38806 18266
Staithe Road, Ludham, NR29 5AB

MARTHAM St Mary

Large enough to have been called 'The cathedral of the Fleggs', (the word Flegg is of Scandinavian origin meaning flat, which exactly describes the local area). Possibly the most notable feature of the church is the Seven Sacrament font – Norfolk has 25 of the 40 in England).

Grid Ref: TG 45497 18442
Black Street, Martham, NR29 4PR

MELTON CONSTABLE St Peter

This quaint and orderly little church is situated in the grounds of Melton Constable Hall, country seat of the Astley Family. It was the Royalist commander Sir Jacob Astley who, before the Battle of Edgehill prayed, 'O Lord, Thou knowest how busy I must be this day; if I forget Thee, do not Thou forget me'.

The Norman tower divides the nave and chancel. The south transept contains the Hastings pew with a staircase leading to it – Hastings is the ennobled Astley name.

Grid Ref: TG 03783 31961
The Street, Melton Constable, NR24 2NE

MORNINGTHORPE St John the Baptist

Probably the round tower was begun before the Norman Conquest. The rest of the church is 14th century, although the roofs of the nave and chancel are Victorian. The royal arms of George III hang above the south door and again, for good measure, they hang over the tower arch. The latter are handsomely carved from a single block of oak. Below them stands the 15th century font with lions and angels one of whom wears a bonnet in 15th century fashion. Altogether a pretty little church.

Grid Ref: TM 22741 93289
The Street, Morningthorpe, NR15 2QU

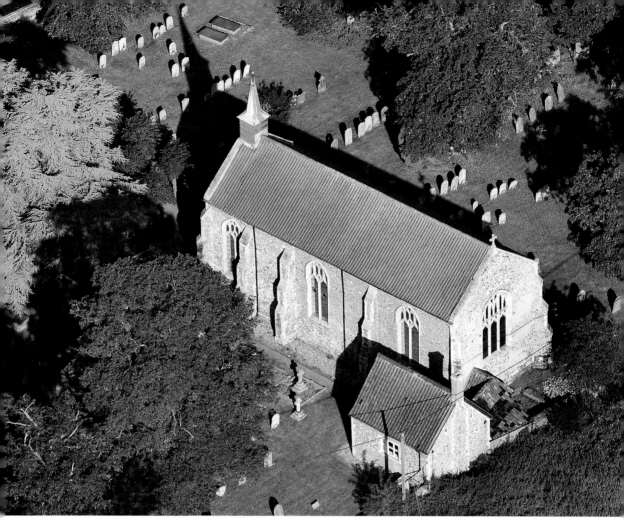

NEATISHEAD St Peter

What is here is the chancel of the original, larger church (rebuilt 1790) which explains its regular shape.

Grid Ref: TG 34465 19735
Church Road, Neatishead, NR12 8BT

NECTON All Saints

The tower is topped by a rather decorative lantern but the tower itself is worthy of special attention – it looks part of the English Gothic order of architecture (1335-50) but in fact it was built in 1865! The rest of the church is genuine Early English. The angels in the roof are what makes this church extra special – rather a lot of them, large and small, and beautifully carved. Restoration on the roof some years ago revealed on the top of a beam, where no one could possibly have seen it, a beautifully carved mouse – truly a labour of love.

Grid Ref: TF 87848 09755
Tuns Road, Necton, PE37 8HE

NORTH CREAKE St Mary

The Victorians, with their usual zeal and energy, made their mark on this church although some monuments and other artefacts were left 'unimproved'. One such was the Easter Sepulchre, believed to be one of only eight in Norfolk (others are at Blakeney, Kelling, Woodrising, Scoulton, Martham, Northwold and Wiveton). Made of soft material, possibly chalk, the sepulchre traditionally stood on the north wall of the chancel and played a significant role in pre Reformation Easter ritual. In *England's Thousand Best Churches* Simon Jenkins is rather sniffy about the angels on the hammerbeams, describing them as 'gaudy'.

Grid Ref: TF 85409 37730
Church Street, North Creake, NR21 9JJ

NORTH ELMHAM St Mary

The ruins of a Saxon cathedral stand within a stone's throw of the church. The bench ends are 'a jolly menagerie of odd birds and beasts, including a muzzled little fellow who presumably is a bear'. During the elimination of references to 'graven images' (usually faces) during the Reformation, the rood screen with saints in a line was pulled out and laid upside down – literally 'face down' in this instance – as pew flooring. It was rediscovered and reinstalled in its rightful place in 19th century. At the Reformation North Elmham church was quick to remove its idolatrous glass pictures and in 1542 Sir John Elveriche paid six shillings and eight pence 'towarde the making of ye mydle panes of the gret window yn (in) Seynt James Chapell wit whyte glasse'.

Grid Ref: TF 98818 21507
Holt Road, North Elmham, NR20 5JU

NORTH LOPHAM St Nicholas

In 1479 Thomas Gentre left money to build the tower and nine others followed
his example. The initials of some of them appear on the tower's south face. In
1486 John and Alice Barker left money for the same purpose asking also that
their souls be prayed for. They all got their tower in 1526; good things come
to those who wait.

Grid Ref: TM 03628 82550
Church Road, North Lopham, IP22 2LP

NORTHREPPS St Mary

The 15th century tower is described as 'a compact design with good detail'. The rood screen was rescued, presumably from those who came to destroy its graven images. It was hidden in a barn and returned. Appropriately in this rural area in the base of the tower there's a plough of the type which was in common use throughout 19th century Norfolk, it was made at the local foundry.

Grid Ref: TG 24455 39066
Church Street, Northrepps, NR27 0LG

Norwich churches

In the 17th century there was, in Norwich, a church for every week of the year and a pub for every day. But a century earlier it has been claimed that there were 500 pubs and 63 churches. There are today only 31 churches still standing of which eight are in use as parish churches, eight are in the care of the Norwich Historic Churches Trust, three in the care of the Churches Conservation Trust and one in private ownership. The major closures took place after the Reformation . Four were lost to enemy bombing in the Second World War of which only St Julian's was rebuilt. There is no 'Early English' style in the Norwich churches which is why the Duke of Norfolk specified the style for the new Roman Catholic church (now cathedral).

NORWICH
The Holy and Undivided Trinity –
Norwich Anglican Cathedral

The cathedral sits in the lower, older, part of the city close to the River Wensum but because the spire is 315 feet high glimpses of it can be seen on several approach roads. The proximity of the river was an important factor for Bishop Herbert de Losinga in deciding on a site. Work began in 1096 using stone from Caen in Normandy and Barnack near Peterborough. The stone was brought by river as far as Pulls Ferry and transhipped through the Close by a canal, of which no trace remains.

Grid Ref: TG 23501 08917
Bishopgate, Norwich, NR1 4EH

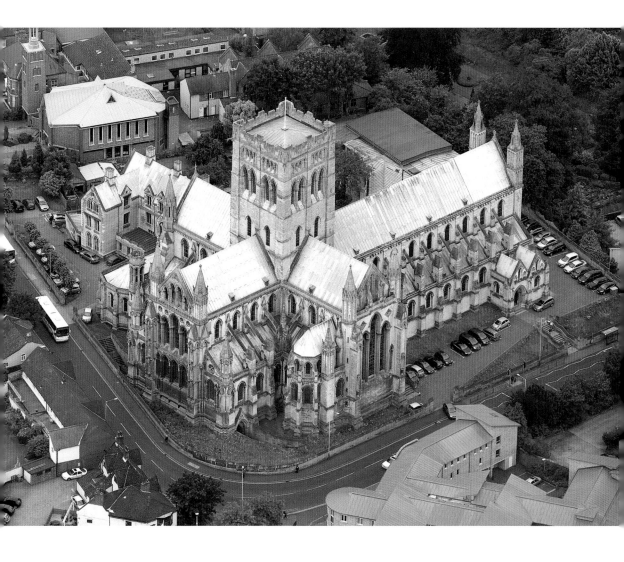

NORWICH
St John the Baptist Roman Catholic Cathedral

Begun in 1884 on the site of the former city gaol this was built as a parish church and didn't attain cathedral status until 1976. It's the second largest Roman Catholic cathedral in England (the largest is Westminster Cathedral – not to be confused with Westminster Abbey). It was funded by the Duke of Norfolk, designed by George Gilbert Scott Jnr and completed by his brother John Oldrid Scott when mental illness prevented George from completing the building. By contrast with the low lying ground on which the Anglican Cathedral stands this building is in one of the highest parts of the city.

Grid Ref: TG 22356 08547
Unthank Road, Norwich, NR2 2RA

NORWICH St John de Sepulchre

Finkelgate is Viking for 'a curving street' (although the little that remains today is only slightly curved). There was a church here by 1066 but the present one dates from 1472 and has one of the most beautiful towers in Norwich. The flint flushwork parapet and pinnacles date from 1901. The font has crouching lions on alternate panels and is similar to several other Norfolk fonts – the lion was a mediaeval symbol of the resurrection. There's also a richly decorated reredos (altar screen) of 1914 by John Oldrid Scott. This church became redundant in 1984 and for some years afterwards was used by an Eastern Orthodox congregation.

Grid Ref: TG 23466 07762
Ber Street, Norwich, NR1 3HD

NORWICH St Clement

St Clements is thought to be one of the first of the Norwich churches built north of the river, possibly as early as 1040. It's surrounded on all sides by footpaths, a characteristic of important Anglo Saxon churches. Churches nearby paid tithes to St Clements indicating that it might have had parish church status. After it was declared redundant in the 1960s the Reverend Jack Burton (a Norwich bus driver and ordained Methodist worker-priest) eventually took over the church and paid rent to the Norwich Historic Churches Trust for over 30 years, opening it for private prayer and meditation. Matthew Parker, Archbishop of Canterbury during Elizabeth I's reign, was educated by the Rector of St Clements. He acquired the epithet of 'Nosey Parker' because of his 'investigative attitude' to matters in general.

Grid Ref: TG 23180 09045
St Clements Abbey, Norwich, NR3 1HZ

NORWICH St Giles-on-the-Hill

St Giles has the highest tower (113 feet) of all the Norwich churches and it is in the highest part of the city. In 1549 a beacon was placed on the top of the tower to guide travellers across the marshy ground from the river Wensum. The cresset (the iron fire basket) is now on view in the church and was replaced by the present cupola in 1737. A stunning sight in late spring are the flowering standard wisterias in the churchyard bordering St Giles' Street.

Grid Ref: TG 22565 08600
St Giles Street, Norwich, NR2 1EZ

NORWICH St John Maddermarket

Madder is a dye and it's probable that the area is named after markets held here. The church has a truncated appearance because there's no external division between nave and chancel. Looking from above at the density of old houses surrounding the church and churchyard it's not difficult to imagine the quality of the drinking water here before Victorian sanitation....'pure eau de churchyard!' A plaque commemorates the feat of actor Will Kemp who had a wager with his friend William Shakespeare that he (Kemp) could Morris dance all the way from London to Norwich. On arrival he jumped the wall of St John's churchyard. Show-off!

Grid Ref: TG 22936 08667
St John Maddermarket, Norwich, NR2 1DQ

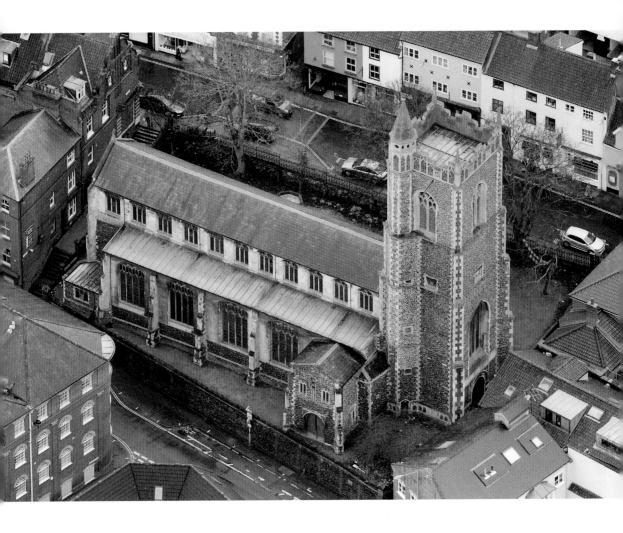

NORWICH St Lawrence

The church stands dramatically on a steep slope. Its most prominent feature is the tower with corner turret. From 1811-27 its curate was Edward Glover, father of Sarah Glover who invented the tonic sol-fa method of singing. The church closed in 1968 at which time there was talk of removing its roof to become a 'controlled ruin' (see also Wiggenhall St Peter) but in 1992 it was taken into the Churches Conservation Trust.

Grid Ref: TG 22747 08788
St Benedicts St and Westwick St, Norwich, NR13 3PL

NORWICH St Miles

Approaching from Duke Street the wonderful flint flushwork of the east wall is inspiring. The church is now redundant and for several years after deconsecration was a popular Science Discovery Centre

Grid Ref: TG 22828 08994
Colegate, Norwich, NR3 3DU

NORWICH St Peter Mancroft

This is the city's parish church. Begun in 1430 it stands high above the market place. An impressive feature is the run of 17 windows in the clerestory. Top of the tower is a 'spike' (Pevsner) with 'dainty flying buttresses' (Pevsner again) giving a total spire height of 146 feet.

Grid Ref: TG 22925 08427
Millennium Plain, Norwich, NR2 1QZ

NORWICH St Stephen

An unusual feature of this church is that the tower stands on the north side and is an upwards continuation of the porch. In 1648 the 'Great Blow' from an exploding arsenal in Bethel Street shattered all the windows in the area. When St Stephen's East Window was restored it contained five large figures of 1511 from the Mariawald monastery on the Ruhr and a jigsaw of small pieces from the original window. Windows again were shattered during the Second World War when Norwich suffered the Baedecker Raids of April 1942. St Stephen's was the last of the great mediaeval churches to be built in the city.

Grid Ref: TG 22918 08297
Rampant Horse Street, Norwich, NR2 1QP

ORMESBY St Margaret

The tower is described as 'good looking' having stepped battlements and a decorative base course. The Lacon mausoleum north of the church and off picture has been described as 'looming like a wartime bunker, surmounted by an uncompromising cross'.

Grid Ref: TG 49882 14531
Yarmouth Road, Ormesby St Margaret, NR29 3QD

ORMESBY St Michael

This is an obviously well cared for church. The 14th century tower, together with the rest of the church, was restored fairly recently. The royal arms are those of our present Queen Elizabeth II. In 2009 the east window depicting Madonna and Child was chosen by Royal Mail as the Christmas First Class stamp design.

Grid Ref: TG 48072 14884
Main Road, Ormesby St Michael, NR29 3LN

OXBOROUGH St John Evangelist

Oxburgh Hall (National Trust) uses the alternate spelling.

The tower with spire (one of only two mediaeval stone spires in Norfolk) collapsed in 1948, bringing with it the nave roof and most of the south side of the nave, so the chancel became the church. Within the part ruined church there's an intact chapel, the Bedingfield Chapel, where magnificent terracotta tombs of the Bedingfield family lie. Sir Edmund Bedingfield built the Hall in 1482; the Bedingfields of Oxburgh Hall are still resident today, nearly six centuries later.

Grid Ref: TF 74413 01451
The Street, Oxburgh, PE33 9PS

PANXWORTH All Saints

Having become redundant in the 1970s the rest of the church was demolished by order of the Church Commissioners to avoid vandalism but the mediaeval tower was allowed to remain.

Grid Ref: TG 34749 13566
Church Road, Panxworth, NR13 6JF

POTTER HEIGHAM St Nicholas

The 12th century round tower with embattlements is regarded as one of the finest in the county. Inside the church there's an unusual 15th century font, it's made of brick rather than the more usual stone. And those bricks are said to have been made from the clay pit in the village. The faces on the rood screen have been scratched out, the work of the iconoclasts of Oliver Cromwell's reign.

The November 2011 picture (right) shows the church with a thatched roof which by July 2013 had been replaced (above) with a metal one.

Grid Ref: TG 41944 19930
Church Lane, Potter Heigham, NR29 5LL

PUDDING NORTON St Margaret

The village and church (12th or 13th century) were deserted by 1602. All that remains is part of the tower and fragments of the nave. Aerial photography reveals earthworks showing streets of what was once a thriving community. Whilst it isn't known for certain why the village was abandoned, it's possible that with the shift from arable to the more profitable sheep husbandry in the Middle Ages the population was driven away by the landowner, much as villagers were during the Highland Clearances. The Black Death may have taken its toll here as elsewhere or there may have been a drift of population into the towns. And the quaint place name? Norton is a corruption of north, Pudding or Pudden is an old word for a toad (as in the marshy area called Puddingmoor in Beccles). Toads live in damp places, sheep don't like damp places – they get foot rot and fail to thrive ,so perhaps it wasn't such a brilliant idea after all to drive out the arable tenants of Pudding Norton and abandon the church so that it fell down.

Grid Ref: TF 92245 27759
B1146, Pudding Norton, NR21 7NB

PULHAM ST MARY St Mary the Virgin

The 15th century stonework on the two storeyed porch is magnificent. There are heraldic beasts at each of the four corners of the parapet, angels playing musical instruments, heraldic shields and stone tracery – all described as 'phenomenal' by Pevsner, a man who didn't exaggerate. The rest of the church is magnificent too.

Grid Ref: TM 21230 85274
The Street, Pulham St Mary, IP21 4RD

QUIDENHAM St Andrew

'Picturesque' properly describes this church. The Anglo Saxon round tower is topped by a Perpendicular upper section and a shingled spire. Spires are less common on Norfolk churches, particularly in the east of the county. The nave and chancel are both of the 14th century although the roofs are modern. The interior is made dark by much Victorian glass and there's a poor box dated 1639, with three locks!

Grid Ref: TM 02836 87674
The Street, Quidenham, NR16 2PJ

RANWORTH St Helen

It's well worth the climb to the top of the tower to get a marvellous view of both Malthouse and Ranworth Broads and beyond. Ranworth is the inner broad where sunken wherries lie. Back safely on the ground, the illustrated rood screen of 1450, the most complete in the county, runs the width of the church and displays the 12 apostles at their most flamboyant, especially St Michael in feathered tunic. Their portrayal provides an insight into the mediaeval mind and the mystery plays of the period. Among the lesser saints stands St George with a defeated dragon and St Michael appears again, this time with a seven headed dragon. There's even a child playing with a toy windmill. A visual feast and that's before the illuminated manuscript (the antiphoner of 1400) has been examined. Made by the monks of Langley Abbey it disappeared in 1552 but was found in a bookshop in 1912. Taken from the manuscript there's a postcard of Jonah half in and half out of the whale on sale at the book stand. And if all of these treasures aren't enough there's a very good tea shop in the churchyard.

Grid Ref: TG 35592 14769
Broad Road, Ranworth, NR13 6HS

RAVENINGHAM St Andrew

In common with large estates (see Felbrigg and Blickling) the church was taken into the park of Raveningham Hall but with public access. The church's round Norman tower predated the Hall by four centuries. Norfolk is very fortunate to have a durable building material, flint, readily available in the fields but in this church something less robust must have been used because every inch of the nave, chancel and tower, except for the battlemented top, has been covered in a cement render changing the building's whole appearance.

Grid Ref: TM 39787 96401
Beccles Road, Raveningham, NR14 6NS

REDENHALL
The Assumption of the Blessed Virgin Mary

The magnificent 15th century tower with its flint flushwork and octagonal buttresses took 60 years to build. The six feet tall lectern may be unique; it has a double headed eagle.

Grid Ref: TM 26390 84378
The Street, Redenhall, IP20 9QS

REEDHAM St John the Baptist

The village has one of the longest established Christian traditions in Norfolk, St Felix, Bishop of Dunwich, who is credited with bringing Christianity to East Anglia, founded a church here in 7th century. And before that the sea – and the Romans – came. The sea formed a large estuary, the Romans left shards of tiles which were used in the building of the church. There was a disastrous fire here in 1981 leaving the church gutted but superhuman effort ensured the fabric was rebuilt within the year.

Grid Ref: TG 42769 02496
Church Road, Reedham, NR13 3UH

REEPHAM and WHITWELL
St Mary and St Michael

It's unusual to have two churches in one churchyard but here there are three! The ruins, in that state since 1543, are of Hackford church. They lie south of St Michael Whitwell and are hidden behind the trees.

St Michael's (left) is the parish church of Whitwell and is connected to St Mary Reepham via St Michael's chancel and vestry connecting door.

St Michael Reepham's tower is oddly positioned being in front of and halfway along the nave, east of the porch.

Grid Ref: TG 10137 22855
Church Street, Reepham. NR10 4JW

ROLLESBY St George

This church has the tallest of the round towers in Norfolk (66 feet to the top of the pinnacles). There's only one taller anywhere and that's at Mutford, Suffolk.

Grid Ref: TG 44621 15759
Fleggburgh Road, Rollesby, NR29 5HH

RUNHAM St Peter & St Paul

Although from the outside this church with its perpendicular tower appears to be in reasonable condition in fact the interior is fast deteriorating, plaster is peeling from the walls, birds have invaded the space and much church furniture has been removed. Pity.

Grid Ref: TG 45981 10827
Church Lane, Herringby, NR29 3EL

SALLE St Peter & St Paul

A magnificent church by anyone's standards and described as Norfolk's rural cathedral. It was built on wool fortunes about AD1400. Rather than using local Norfolk flint the church is built of the more costly Barnack stone. The entrance is through the tower, giving a magnificent view of the nave and chancel as one enters. The roof of St James's Guild Chapel in the south transept is said to be the model for the House of Lords roof. The Seven Sacrament font is considered one of the best in Norfolk and has an impressive font cover. Seven Sacrament fonts were mainly confined to Norfolk and even here they are rare. The seven panels represent the seven ordinances of Baptism, Holy Communion, Confirmation, Confession, Ordination to Holy Orders, Marriage and Anointing of the Dying. The subject of the eighth panel varies and might be, for example, the Baptism of Christ. There's a three decker pulpit, original choir stalls with misericords, window portraits of three cardinals in their wide hats, and 160 angels. A 'must see'.

Grid Ref: TG 11035 24893
The Street, Salle, NR10 4SE

SALTHOUSE St Nicholas

The church stands sensibly, if gaunt, above flood level for the village has suffered many inundations from the sea, spectacularly in 1953. Bored mediaeval choirboys scratched images of sailing ships on the choir stalls.

Grid Ref: TG 07613 43680
The Street, Salthouse, NR25 7XQ

SANDRINGHAM St Mary Magdalene

This small village church is well known to loyal subjects everywhere as the church from which the royal family emerges on Christmas Day. The carstone original was built in the 14th and 15th centuries but was heavily restored from the 1850s onwards with the Prince of Wales (the future King Edward VII) occupying the renovated and remodelled Sandringham House from 1870. Inside, the colours of the Norfolk Regiment hang above the font at the base of the tower. The church is full of gifts from rich foreign dignitaries including a silver altar presented in memory of Edward VII in 1911 and an oak pulpit presented to Queen Alexandra to mark her 80th birthday in 1924.

Grid Ref: TF 69112 28593
Sandringham, PE35 6EH

SEETHING St Margaret & St Remigius

Wilhelmine Harrod, founder of the Norfolk Churches Trust and compiler of the comprehensive and invaluable *Norfolk Guide* writes of Seething church, 'is as nice as its name'. Built over several centuries beginning with its Norman round tower, the church contains several wall paintings, including one of St Christopher, patron saint of travellers. Very apt as many of Seething's Second World War temporary American residents serving in the 8th US Air Force at nearby RAF Seething flew missions to Germany December 1943 – April 1945. 350 of those men were killed in action; a memorial to them stands in the churchyard.

Grid Ref: TM 31969 97948
Brooke Road, Seething, NR15 1DL

SHELFANGER All Saints

The chequered flushwork battlements and pyramidal roof nicely 'finish off' this attractive little country church. Restoration work in the 1960s revealed a five feet high and four feet wide wall painting behind a hollow wall in the chancel. The subject was the Visit of the Magi painted in 13th century. Because it was unexposed for so many centuries its condition remains good.

Grid Ref: TM 10733 83661
Church Road, Shelfanger, IP22 2DU

SHELTON St Mary

The oldest part is the flint tower but the rest of this visually appealing church is of red brick, except for the stone work surrounding the run of nine windows of the clerestory (clear storey). Shelton Hall and the church were built simultaneously by Sir Ralph Shelton but unlucky family links caused further development to stop. His son had married the aunt of Henry VIII's second wife Anne Boleyn and when that unfortunate queen was beheaded her daughter, the future Elizabeth I, fled to Shelton Hall. She sought refuge in the church tower when her life was in danger.

Grid Ref: TM 22097 91045
Low Road, Shelton, NR15 2SD

SHIPDHAM All Saints

'A touch of fancy which crowns the tower like a bit of old Russia' (Mortlock) certainly makes the church distinctive! But recycling seems to be the order of the day here. A Norman font was discovered 30 years ago in the rectory garden (whatever was it used for?) and returned to the church together with a board on which the royal arms for Charles I 1630 were painted, updated for Charles II in 1661. In the north aisle there's a mediaeval chest with five locks. Many churches still have their parish chests and today they're an important tool of social history. In 1538 by order of Thomas Cromwell (Henry VIII's vicar general) parish registers containing the names of those christened, married and died within each parish were to be kept, although their reliability depended on the diligence of each parish priest. The register was to be kept in a locked chest, but five locks?!

Grid Ref: TF 95793 07358
New Road, Shipdham, IP25 7JX

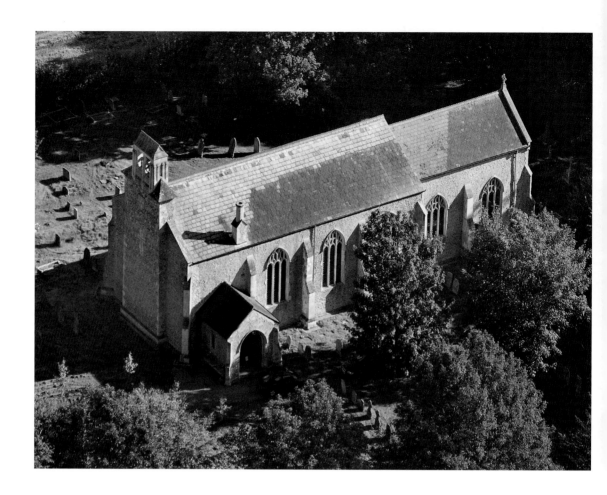

SMALLBURGH St Peter

The tower fell in 1677, taking with it part of the nave. This was replaced in 1902 when the bell cote was added.

Grid Ref: TG 33372 23959
Hall Road, Smallburgh, NR12 9NB

SNETTISHAM St Mary

In Norfolk, churches with spires are few and they tend to be, as is this one, in the west of the county. The spire is 175 feet high and was rebuilt in 1895. The church beneath it is mainly 14th century with some later work. It has the 'distinction' of being the first church in England to be bombed from the air – the east window was blown in by a Zeppelin raid in 1915.

Grid Ref: TF 69054 34277
Old Church Road, Snettisham, PE31 7NA

SOUTHBURGH St Andrew

Sited in the rural area of Breckland this church would look more at home in an urban setting. Are the tower buttresses necessary to stabilise this relatively short tower or is it a piece of overkill of which the Victorians were sometimes guilty? There remain little bits of the 13th and 14th century original but this is mainly a Victorian restoration.

Grid Ref: TG 00314 04833
Church Lane, Southburgh, IP25 7TF

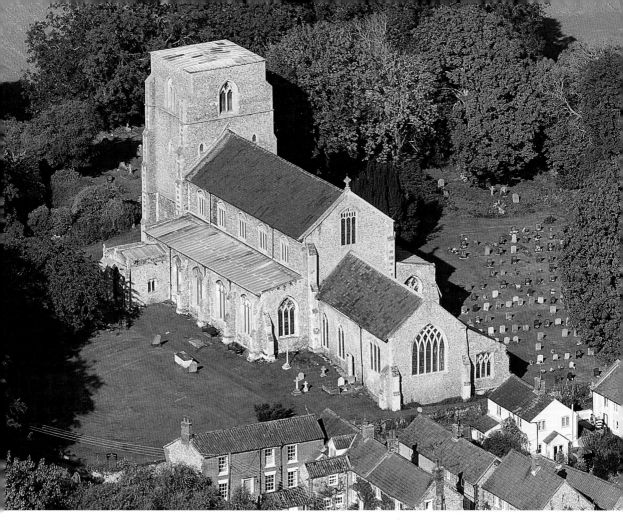

SOUTH CREAKE St Mary the Virgin

The tower is early 14th century and has an unfinished look – it seems to need a parapet, actually it had one once and bits of it can now be found in the churchyard wall. Parapets often were added centuries later and in styles more ornate than the rest of the church. Inside are 22 angels – some with repaired wings, a wineglass pulpit, traces of the space for an Easter Sepulchre, a Seven Sacrament font and in the spandrels (the triangular space between the curve of an arch and the roof) a dragon, a unicorn and a pelican. Well worth a visit.

Grid Ref: TF 85526 36230
Church Lane, South Creake, NR21 9LX

SOUTH LOPHAM St Andrew

Quoted as being 'one of the grandest pieces of Norman architecture in the county'. The central tower with its blind arcading rises to 100 feet. It was part of a church which William Bigod, son of Roger who came over with William the Conqueror, gave to the monks of Thetford. Elements of Saxon building within the church suggest that the tower was built onto an older Saxon building. Inside there's a huge chest carved from a single piece of tree trunk which is believed to be as old as the tower itself. Some of the pew ends contain intricate carvings; one is an Elephant & Castle, others have 'grotesques' and figures.

Grid Ref: TM 03963 81756
Church Road, South Lopham, IP22 2LW

STRUMPSHAW St Peter

The 15th century tower has a 'flourish' of eight pinnacles.

Little did this wedding party realise they would go down in history in a way they hadn't expected!

Grid Ref: TG 34921 07724
Norwich Road, Strumpshaw, NR13 4NR

SURLINGHAM St Mary

The four bells were restored and two more added to ring in the millennium! The chancel was restored circa 1880 but why in red brick? Norfolk red brick is notoriously soft, flint to match the rest of the church is readily available. Inside,

a lectern in silvery oak was presented in 1969. There's the traditional lectern eagle, wings outstretched to support the bible but an owl sits beneath the eagle's feet. Scary for the owl.

Grid Ref: TG 30584 06516
Church Lane, Surlingham, NR14 7DF

SWAFFHAM St Peter and St Paul

The spike (cupola) on the top of the Barnack stone tower (the tower built 1510, slightly later than the church) is distinctive and inside the church there are other features which make this particularly interesting. There are angels, 88 of them in the chestnut double hammerbeam roof (apparently chestnut wood doesn't attract as much dust as some woods) and they're peppered with gunshot. Not, as one would expect, fired by iconoclasts but by shooting parties aiming to rid the roof of nesting birds. A pew end contains the figure of John Chapman, supposedly a pedlar and benefactor of the church. The story goes that on London Bridge he was told to return to Swaffham and dig in his garden where he would find a crock of gold – an unlikely story but a nice one. He was wealthy enough (crock of gold or not) to finance the rebuilding of some of the church. John Chapman's dog features with him on the pew end and also outside on the porch gable.

Grid Ref: TF 82070 08999
Mangate Street, Swaffham, PE37 7QN

SWARDESTON St Mary the Virgin

This is an attractive church in a pleasant south Norfolk village but it might go unremarked but for Nurse Edith Cavell 1865-1915. Her father was vicar here for almost 50 years and she was born here. She was shot by the Germans in occupied Belgium for hiding allied soldiers and enabling their escapes. Her words on the eve of her execution have gone down in history:

"Standing, as I do, in view of God and eternity I realise that patriotism is not enough. I must have no hatred or bitterness towards anyone."

In Swardeston church she is commemorated by a stained glass window and an annual service on a date near to her execution but she is known more widely from her statue in Norwich's Tombland. She's buried in Life's Green in the Cathedral grounds.

Grid Ref: TG 19897 02400
The Street, Swardeston, NR14 8DG

TASBURGH St Mary

The Iron Age fort built and occupied here between 600BC and AD100 later provided a safe site for the establishment of this church, which is Saxon (5th and 6th century) in origin. The round tower reinforces the debatable theory that the tower, much like the fort, was a defensive structure. It sits in the centre of the hill fort site.

Grid Ref: TM 20111 95888
Church Hill, Tasburgh, NR15 1NH

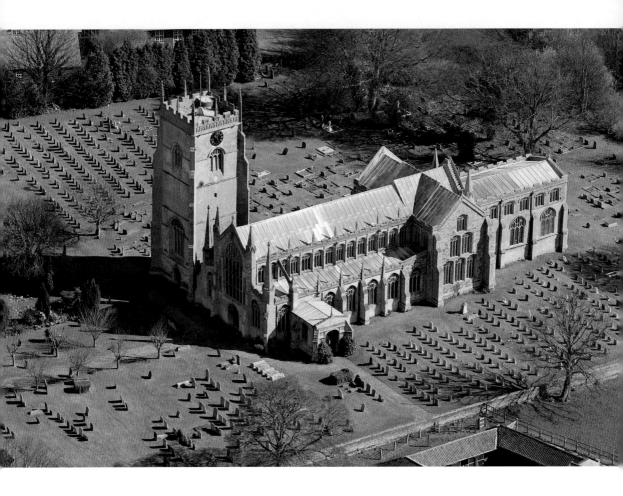

TERRINGTON ST CLEMENT St Clement

During 14th century the area was prosperous as is reflected in some of the most magnificent churches in Norfolk. This one has been termed, 'the Cathedral of the Marshes'. Built of Barnack stone which would have been relatively easy to transport along Fenland waters, those waterways can prove also to be a hazard, for instance in 1607 when a dyke burst and villagers had to flee to the church tower for safety. The last dyke wall to be built round here was constructed by German prisoners of war during the period 1914-18. And of the many treasures in the church the royal arms of Queen Anne and the Lord's Prayer board of 1635 are outstanding.

Grid Ref: TF 55196 20440
Churchgate Way, Terrington St Clements, PE34 4LZ

THORNHAM All Saints

Described as 'a well proportioned, rather good looking church', it was built in the largely Perpendicular style with a plain tower and a two storey porch. There's a fragment of wall painting on the west wall – before the Reformation churches contained much decoration, especially wall paintings. The rood screen (dated 1488) is particularly fine, if faded. And some of the poppy heads on the pew ends cause wry amusement; there's a fox in priest's clothing with a couple of geese sticking out from under his habit (a mediaeval way of poking fun at the clergy).

Grid Ref: TF 73364 43446
Church Street, Thornham, PE36 6NJ

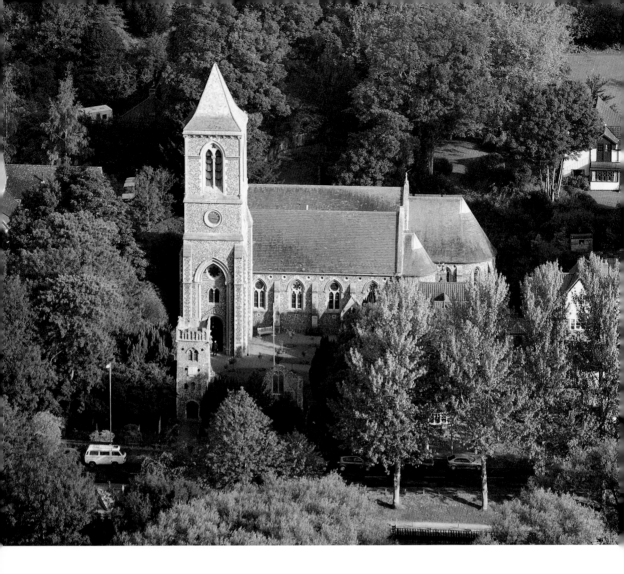

THORPE EPISCOPI St Andrew

There are several 'thorpes' in Norfolk. The word denotes a Danish settlement. This one, a suburb of Norwich, is best known as Thorpe St Andrew. The tower standing alone by the roadside is all that remains of a mediaeval church, the rest was demolished in the 1880s. The spire of the new church originally was 150 feet high, but was bomb damaged in 1944, and the pyramid top replaces it. Entry into the church is through the tower. Inside there's a 20th century rood screen of 15th century design but instead of the customary saints as decoration there are figures such as the Bishop of Lincoln, a Victoria Cross holder and an American actress who as far as anyone can tell has no connection whatsoever with the church. It wouldn't happen today!

Grid Ref: TG 26067 08412
Yarmouth Road, Thorpe St Andrew, NR7 0EW

THUXTON All Saints

This small country church has a distinctive 14th century octagonal belfry with an external stair turret leading to it. The royal arms of Charles I dated 1637 were made by a local craftsman. The display of royal coats of arms in the church, either painted on a wooden panel or sculpted in stone, became common during the reign of Henry VIII when he assumed complete control of the English church. Many disappeared by royal command during the short reign of his daughter the Catholic Mary but reappeared with subsequent monarchs. During Oliver Cromwell's reign many were destroyed by order.

Grid Ref: TG 03242 07106
Station Lane, Thuxton, NR9 4QL

TITCHWELL St Mary

It is described as 'a tiny picturesque church hugging the edge of the saltmarshes'. The base of the tower is probably Saxon and has large flints unevenly laid at its base. Sympathetic restoration work circa 1900 has left indications of where previous doorways and windows existed. In the churchyard stands Cedric's Oak, grown from an acorn from New Zealand and planted as a memorial to New Zealand's contribution in both world wars.

Grid Ref: TF 76217 43876
Church Lane, Titchwell, PE31 8BA

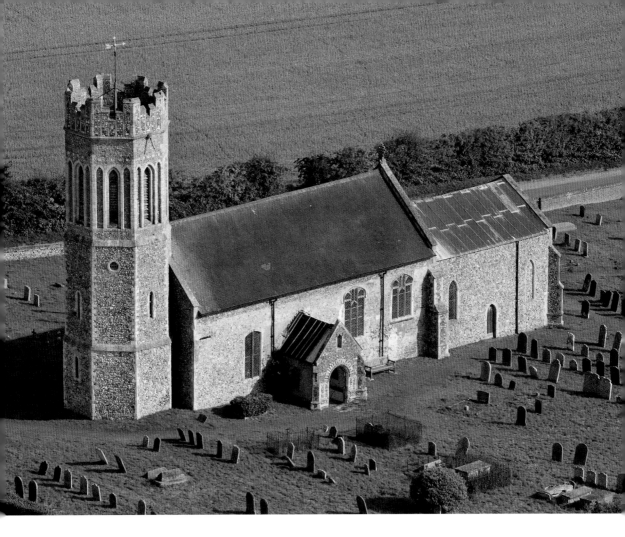

TOFT MONKS St Margaret

'Toft' originally meant the site of a religious house but by the 14th century the only resident here was the prior. He belonged to the order of the Norman Benedictine Abbey of Preaux in France. The fine tower is octagonal from the base upwards but Pevsner, the unsurpassed buildings expert, suggests that underneath the octagonal 13th century shape lies an older Norman structure.

Grid Ref: TM 42625 95268
Pound Lane, Toft Monks, NR34 0ET

TOPCROFT St Margaret

The tower is fascinating, it was built over three periods. The round base is Norman, then in the 13th century upper part of the round tower was replaced by this octagonal stage with thin brick and tile at the quoins (corners). The flushwork patterns at the top were made in the 15th century. The red brick chancel was rebuilt in 1712.

Grid Ref: TM 26583 92898
Church Road, Topcroft, NR35 2BH

TRUNCH St Botolph

The most magnificent feature in the whole church is the oak font canopy, it's only one of four in England and St Peter Mancroft has one of the others. It contains riotous carvings of flowers, birds and animals, including a pig wearing a bishop's mitre! Font covers came into use to protect the holy water when suspicion arose that it was being stolen for use in witchcraft.

Grid Ref: TG 28711 34857
North Walsham Road, Trunch, NR28 0PS

UPPER SHERINGHAM All Saints

The mediaeval bench ends are well worth a special visit. The fine carvings show a griffin, a monkey, dragon, a chrysom (a cloth wrapping a stillborn or newly born child whose mother had not yet been 'churched' i.e. been to church to give thanks), a cat with a mouse, heraldic beasts and best known of all and nearest the south door for a quick exit, a mermaid. Legend has it she slithered from the sea – at least a mile distant – perched on the end of the nearest pew then slithered back to the sea when admonished for being in the church at all – an unlikely tale. The circular pond-like structure on the edge of the churchyard is a drinking water reservoir for horses. Near the north door in the churchyard stands a sad reminder, a granite memorial to the crew of a USAAF Liberator which on January 4 1944 crashed nearby whilst returning from a mission to Kiel.

Grid Ref: TG 14362 41925
Limekiln Lane, Upper Sheringham, NR26 8UB

WALPOLE ST ANDREW St Andrew

It is described as 'one of the big Marshland churches' along with Walpole St Peter and the Terringtons, both St Clement and St John. The construction is mainly of brick with stone facings. The erosion of the plaster rendering , revealing brickwork in the nave, may be explained by the roof having been removed for some long while prior to renovation. The tower may have been a shrine for pilgrims praying for a safe passage before setting out across the treacherous marshes to Lincolnshire – it was in this parish in 1216 that King John's retinue lost his jewels attempting the crossing to Long Sutton......or were the jewels stolen? They've never been found. In the north aisle are two shepherds' crooks as a reminder of the Shepherds' Club founded in 1841, 'to relieve the sick, bury the dead and assist each other in all cases of unavoidable distress'. Pity King John wasn't a member of a Club like that.

Grid Ref: TF 50162 17558
Kirk Road, Walpole St Andrew, PE14 7LN

WALPOLE ST PETER St Peter

This is one of Simon Jenkins' *England's Thousand Best Churches*, being richly decorated and massive. The tower (built 1300AD) is plainer than the rest of the building because it was the only part of the original building to survive the great flood of 1337. Ten years after the Black Death (1348) rebuilding began; the chancel was added in 1420 and the south porch 30 years later. There's an underground passage which runs under the church to the edge of the churchyard so that processions could stay within consecrated ground. One of the roof bosses in the passage is a sheep's head; that's a clue as to where the money to build came from, much like Worstead and the great Suffolk churches of Lavenham and Long Melford.

Grid Ref: TF 50215 16882
Church Road, Walpole St Peter, PE14 7NS

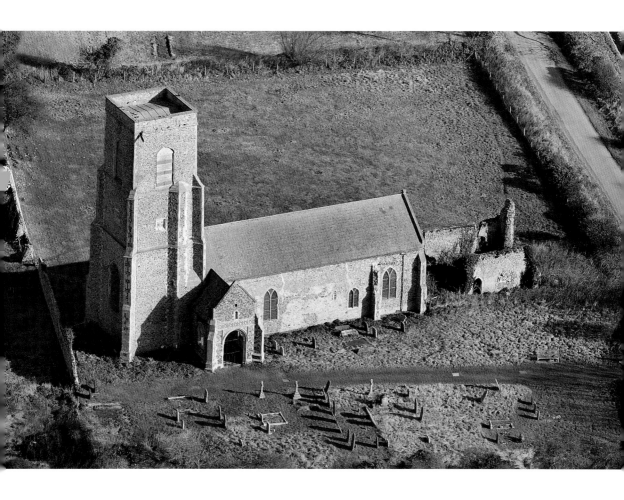

WAXHAM St John

This is a sad little church. Damp pervades the interior, weeds grow in the churchyard. The Decalogue board installed by order of Elizabeth I displaying the ten commandments is one of the few signs that a congregation ever sat here reading them.

Grid Ref: TG 44053 26232
Church Road, Waxham, NR12 0DY

WESTON LONGVILLE All Saints

Best known as Parson Woodforde's church, although it had been standing for several centuries when he was appointed in 1760. He kept a diary for the next 43 years until his death and that diary is the chronicle of a country parson whose interest seems to have centred mainly on meals.

Grid Ref: TG 11339 15865
Church Road, Weston Longville, NR9 5JU

WEST RUNTON Holy Trinity

East and West Runton comprise one parish. The church is undoubtedly the oldest building in a parish which contains rather a lot of cliff top caravans. The tower dates from the 12th century, the rest is slightly later. The font is similar to those at nearby Roughton and Sheringham.

Grid Ref: TG 17959 42832
Cromer Road, West Runton, NR27 9QT

WEST SOMERTON St Mary

It's a temptation to be resisted to be so busy in the churchyard seeking out the grave of the 'Norfolk Giant' that the beauty of this church is missed. It's a little gem. Onto the round tower an octagonal top was added in the 14th century and the whole was restored to commemorate the millennium. A Norman doorway on the south side of the thatched nave was built somewhere between 1066 and 1200. Robert Hales....was seven feet eight inches tall and weighed 33 stones (his sister was seven feet three inches tall). His huge inscribed tomb is easy to find in the north-east corner of the churchyard.

Grid Ref: TG 47540 19547
Church Road, Somerton, NR29 4DR

WEYBOURNE All Saints

The ruins of a 13th century Augustinian priory are adjacent giving a timeless feel to the whole. In the nave there's a notice pointing out that all the poppy heads (at the end of pews) were carved circa 1900 by three sisters. They're expertly done and demonstrate of skills of Victorian ladies or rather those Victorian ladies lucky enough to have leisure time in which to learn and practise decorative skills.

Grid Ref: TG 11163 43032
The Street, Weybourne, NR25 7SX

WHEATACRE All Saints

The chequer boarded brick and flint pattern on the 16th century tower is unusual, even in this area.

Grid Ref: TM 46055 93943
Church Road, Wheatacre, NR34 0AU

WICKHAMPTON St Andrew

The church is adjacent to the marshes which stretch across to Breydon Water. Before the marshes were drained (in the 16th century) and the area was a tidal estuary there was a large community living here – now St Andrew's stands almost alone. An unusual feature is the fact that the tower's four pinnacles each houses a weather vane. Church historians declare that the 14th century wall paintings are outstanding – one of the finest ranges in the country, they cover most of the north wall. Among them 'The Three Living and Three Dead' is an allegorical story from 13th century French Literature where three young courtiers encounter three skeletons. The first skeleton tells the first young man 'As I am so you shall be'. The second and third encounters are in similar vein. Other known examples of this painting in Norfolk are at Paston, Seething and Belton.

Grid Ref: TG 42726 05470
The Street, Wickhampton, NR13 3PB

WICKLEWOOD St Andrew and All Saints

The south door is, uncommonly, part of the tower. And there's unusual brick and flint banding in the wall at the western end of the nave suggesting that this particular wall had fireplaces in the tower. The one on the first floor is 'big enough to roast a pig' (Mortlock and Roberts).

Grid Ref: TG 06976 02338
Hackford Road, Wicklewood, NR18 9QT

WIGGENHALL ST PETER St Peter

Pevsner described this derelict church as, 'an excellent ruin because the walls stand all the way up and only the roofs are gone'. It now stands below the level of the raised banks of the river Ouse.

Grid Ref: TF 60435 13253
St Peters Road, Wiggenhall, PE34 3HF

WINTERTON Holy Trinity and All Saints

The 132 feet tower stood as a landmark for centuries of shipping in the North Sea, just as did Cromer, Happisburgh and Blakeney church towers. The tapering buttresses give a solid feel to the whole. The fine south porch is thought to have been built by Sir John Fastolf of Caister Castle. It wasn't until 14th century that church porches came to be regarded as an essential. Churches built before this don't have them. The baptism and wedding services began here. Geoffrey Chaucer's 'Canterbury Tales' (mid 14th century) says of the 'Wife of Bath'

　　She was a worthy woman al hir lyve
　　Housbands at chirch dore she hadde fyve

Women were 'churched' here (i.e. gave thanks) after the birth of a child and those churches which had an upper floor often were used as school rooms with the parish priest as teacher.

Grid Ref: TG 49117 19462
Black Street, Winterton, NR29 4DB

WITTON by Norwich St Margaret

Instead of a tower this picturesque church has a bell turret. The whole building has been heavily restored but its essential attractiveness has been retained. Originally there was a tower at the west end – a stair turret still exists.

Grid Ref: TG 31421 09715
Hall Road, Witton, NR13 5DN

WIVETON St Mary

Once the River Glaven was a huge estuary and sea going boats tied up against the churchyard walls, the marks are there still. On the opposite side of what once was the estuary and is now the Glaven valley, stands Cley church. It used to be said of Wiveton and Cley – both 14th century churches facing one another across the estuary – that there was great rivalry between the builders and the best flintwork stood where the other church would have to look at it for ever!

Grid Ref: TG 04359 42801
The Street, Wiveton, NR25 7TP

WOLFERTON St Peter

In 1886 the Prince of Wales changed much of this 14th and 15th century carstone church. Since Wolferton was close to the Wash perhaps earlier this had been a travellers' shrine much like the church at Walpole St Andrew.

Princess, later Queen, Alexandra, presented the silver lectern which originally stood in Sandringham church. The royal arms of 1844 which hang above the tower arch were embroidered by the vicar's daughter.

Grid Ref: TF 65714 28183
The Street, Wolferton, PE31 6HD

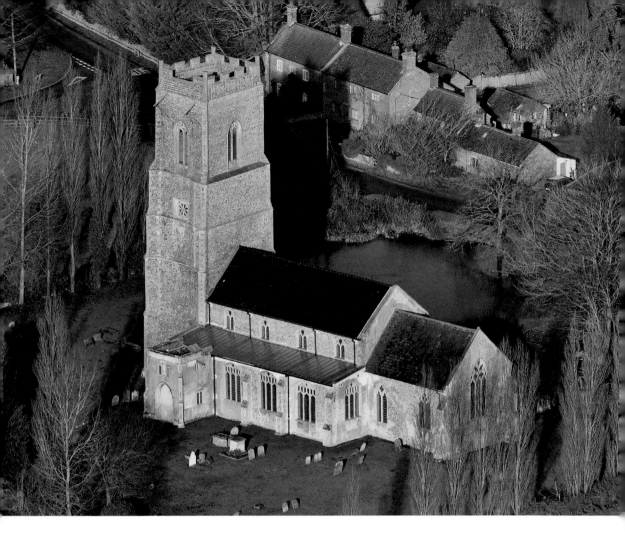

WOOD DALLING St Andrew

The chancel is the oldest part of this church in a delightfully named village whose church is rather larger than its population now can support. Its name originates from the Dalling family, one of whom built the hall in 1592.

Grid Ref: TG 08975 26977
Briston Road, Wood Dalling, NR11 6SN

WOODBASTWICK St Fabian and St Sebastian

There's no other church in England dedicated jointly to these two saints. Woodbastwick is a picturesque village, much photographed. The church contains memorial tablets to the Cator family, lords of the manor. The lych gate, built 1892, is a memorial to Emma Cator.

Grid Ref: TG 33245 15226
Horning Road, Woodbastwick, NR13 6HJ

WOODTON All Saints

Pronounced 'Wuttun' the church's Norman tower has a 15th century top. The Suckling family were lords of the manor here until 1810. In 1749 Catherine Suckling married the Reverend Edmund Nelson of Beccles and later gave birth to England's most famous sailor, Horatio Nelson, at Burnham Thorpe rectory.

Grid Ref: TM 28547 94626
Church Road, Woodton, NR35 2NB

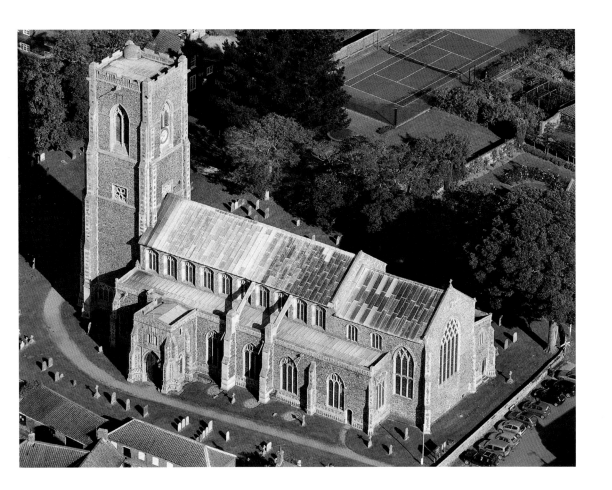

WORSTEAD St Mary

This is one of the magnificent East Anglian churches founded on wool fortunes. Looms worked by members of the Weavers, Spinners and Dyers Guild stand in the north aisle. Before the Reformation many churches had Guilds associated with them. The village gave its name to Worstead cloth. The hammer beam roof was inserted in the 15th century, probably accounting for the flying buttresses over the aisle roofs. The nave has 18th century box pews.

Grid Ref: TG 30194 26060
Front Street, Worstead, NR28 9AL

WRENINGHAM All Saints

Most of the 13th century tower collapsed in 1852 – a church tower collapse is not as uncommon as might be imagined! When it was restored the rest of the church was included. Fortunately the churchyard escaped and it's worth a walk around to see the 18th century headstones, particularly those with cherubs blowing their trumpets with abandon.

Grid Ref: TM 16334 98810
Church Road, Wreningham, NR16 1BH

WROXHAM St Mary

The purpose of the sound holes (the small square openings halfway up the tower) is not as much to let out the sound of the bells into the countryside but to let in light in the ringing chamber and to allow the ringers to hear the bells. In the churchyard stands the pinnacled mausoleum of 1829 of the Trafford family, designed by Anthony Salvin. Salvin went on to remodel the south transept of Norwich Cathedral and worked also on Norwich castle, 'with more enthusiasm than sensibility'. (Mortlock).

Grid Ref: TG 29641 17542
St Mary's Close, Wroxham, NR12 8SG

WYMONDHAM ABBEY St Mary and St Thomas

William d'Albini made a crucial mistake when in 1107 he laid the foundations for the abbey. He planned the huge structure to contain a monastery for 12 monks in one half and a church for Wymondham's parishioners in the other. Over the centuries much bickering went on between the two halves, especially over the bells. This resulted eventually in the great west tower being built to house the parishioners' own bells. The aggro only stopped when Henry VIII hoped to solve his marital difficulties by parting company with the church of Rome and closed all the monasteries. All those monks who agreed to pack up and go received a pension from the king but the bloody minded ones who dug in their heels got nothing. Inevitably the deserted half of the site became the graceful ruins we have today. And if that wasn't unsettling enough, William Kett – brother of people's champion Robert – was hanged from the west tower for his part in a rebellion (1549). Robert Kett was hanged from the battlements of Norwich Castle. On the plus side the Abbey has an impressive reredos screen behind the altar, designed by Ninian Comper as a Great War memorial. And, as with so many of Norfolk's great churches, the roof has loads of angels.

Grid Ref: TG 10688 01498
Church Street, Wymondham, NR18 0PJ

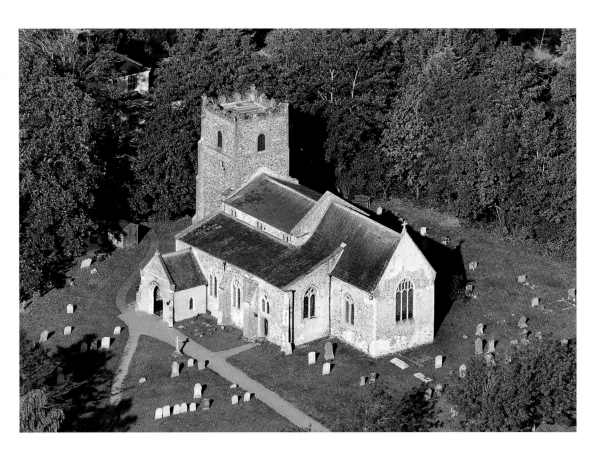

YELVERTON St Mary

Unusually the tower is trimmed with red brick. Presumably this was executed around 1673 when it was rebuilt. The masons' names are on tablets on the tower's south side. The nave roof has been raised to provide three clerestory windows above the three ground level windows. Inside the church is a ledger stone (an inscribed stone laid into the floor) of Anne Rant. Dying in 1698, she had set out in her will that income from land belonging to her in the parish was forever to be divided between the minister and the poor of the parish, 'upon pain of forfeiture of said land'.

Grid Ref: TG 29238 02190
Church Road, Yelverton, NR14 7PB

Bibliography

Chatfield, Mark *Churches the Victorians Forgot* Moorland 1979

Collins *Guide to English Parish Churches* 1958

Dymond, David *The Norfolk Landscape* Alastair Press 1990

Groves, Nicholas *The Mediaeval Churches of the City of Norwich* HEART 2010

Harrod, Wilhemine *The Norfolk Guide* Alastair Press 1988

Hurst, Paul and Haselock, Jeremy *Norfolk Rood Screens* Philimore 2012

Jenkins Simon *England's Thousand Best Churches* Allen Lane 1999

Malster, Robert *Maritime Norfolk Parts One* and *Two* Poppyland 2012 and 2013

Meercs, Frank *Not of this World* Blackall 2001

Messent, Claude, J W *Lych-gates and their churches in Eastern England* 1970

Mortlock and Roberts *Guide to Norfolk Churches* Lutterworth Press 2007

Pevsner, Nikolaus *The Buildings of England North West and South Norfolk* Penguin 1977

Pevsner, Nikolaus *The Buildings of England North East Norfolk and Norwich* Penguin 1977

Pye, Adrian *The Parish Churches of East Norfolk* ASPYE 2010

Pye, Adrian *The Parish Churches of Central Norfolk* ASPYE 2010

Pye, Adrian *The Parish Churches of West Norfolk* ASPYE 2010

Shreeve and Stilgoe *The Round Tower Churches of Norfolk* Canterbury Press 2001

Storey, Neil *The Lost Coast of Norfolk* The History Press 2009

Strong, Roy *A Little History of the English Country Church* Vintage 2007

Taylor, Richard *How to Read a Church* Rider 2003

Tilbrook and Roberts *Norfolk's Churches Great and Small* Jarrold 1997

Index